Endorsements for
Work by Referral. *Live the Good Life!*

Work by Referral. Live the Good Life! is hardly just a book about selling real estate, although no one—no one!—has a more systematic and proven way to do that than Brian Buffini and Joe Niego. It is also a book about how to live a deeply satisfying and meaningful life, and they're just as convincing about how to do that!

> Tony Schwartz, President of The Energy Project, author of
> *The Power of Full Engagement: Managing Energy Not Time*

This book is a must for anyone planning on being highly successful in the real estate business and yet living a happy, well balanced life.

> Wes Foster, Chairman/CEO, Long & Foster Companies

A leader is someone who has a vision, a plan and leads by example. Brian and Joe have experienced great success and they share their plans with you in a well written, entertaining and informative book. The only things that will change you from where you are to where you'll be in five years are the books you read, the people you meet and the dreams you dream. Read this book and it will change your life positively.

> Coach Lou Holtz, former Head Coach, University of
> Notre Dame, inducted in the College Football Hall of Fame

If you are tired and feeling burnt out, this book is a must read. *Work by Referral. Live the Good Life!* will restore and renew your passion, your business, and your life.

> Jack Canfield, author of *The Success Principles*™ and
> co-author of the *Chicken Soup for the Soul*® series

Buffini's commitment to his clients' overall success parallels our own desire to provide an environment that allows our sales associates to improve the quality of their lives and to give back to the communities we serve.

> Lawrence F. (Larry) Flick, IV, Chairman and CEO
> Prudential Fox & Roach, Realtors and The Trident Group

Brian Buffini is one of the world's leading experts on referral marketing. I highly recommend his book *Work by Referral. Live the Good Life!* to anyone who wants to learn how to build their business through the referral process.

    Dr. Ivan Misner, *New York Times* Bestselling author and
    Founder of Business Network International

In today's changing real estate market, having the right game plan in place is critical for success. Brian Buffini's Referral Systems, as clearly outlined in this book, will provide you with a proven strategy for generating a steady stream of business despite market fluctuations.

    John Featherston, CEO & Publisher, RISMedia, publishers of
    Real Estate magazine

Brian Buffini has positively impacted the professional and personal lives of thousands of RE/MAX agents around the world over the past 11 years. This book is the road map to your success; buy it; read it; do it.

    Dave Liniger, Chairman and Co-founder
    RE/MAX International

Brian has synthesized a life's work to give the ultimate roadmap to success as a real estate professional and how to create a meaningful and balanced life. Bravo!! A must read.

    Avram Goldman, President and CEO, Pacific Union GMAC
    Real Estate

Work by Referral. Live the Good Life! lays out a clearly lit path that is easy to follow yet is profound in depth and clarity.

    Jim Rohn, America's foremost business philosopher

Nobody should sell real estate without reading *Work by Referral. Live the Good Life!* This book is insightful, practical, and best of all the strategies are PROVEN.

    Zig Ziglar, author and motivational teacher

I am delighted that Brian and Joe have compiled their systems into a one stop reference to keep me on track! Since I've been following Buffini's Working by Referral program, I feel set free!

    Judy Moses, 2007 National President, Women's Council
    of Realtors

BRIAN BUFFINI
& JOE NIEGO

WORK
By Referral
Live the Good Life!

∼

PROVEN STRATEGIES
FOR SUCCESS AND HAPPINESS
IN THE REAL ESTATE BUSINESS

BUFFINI
& COMPANY ™

Published by Buffini & Company, Inc.
Carlsbad, CA, U.S.A.

100 Days to Greatness, "Oh, by the way . . .," and Turning Point Retreat are registered trademarks of Buffini & Company, Inc. The Turning Point, Buffini & Company Turning Point, ClubNet, Buffini & Company Referral Systems Member, Buffini & Company Certified Mentor, Peak Performers, *Work by Referral. Live the Good Life!*, Client Appreciation Program, and Ultimate Office Kit are trademarks of Buffini & Company, Inc.

ISBN: 978-0-9820260-0-7

Printed in the United States of America

Dedication

To the men and women who have boldly
stepped into the real estate sales and lending arena:
Your courage is inspiring.

You believed in yourself and entered a business
with no guarantee of income, benefits, or support.

We honor you. We salute you. We believe in you.

We hope this book will bring you
encouragement and direction.

Acknowledgements

There is not enough time or space to properly acknowledge all those who have contributed to our success in real estate and happiness in life. You know who you are. Please accept our heartfelt thank you.

A few special thanks ~

To Beverly and Julie: your unconditional love and support is our strength. Often times we talk about how fortunate we are to be married to people like you. You bring so much joy to life.

To our kids, the "A Team" and "Fab 5": thanks for being who you are. When we grow up, we want to be like you. We can't imagine life without you.

To David Lally: thanks for getting this whole project started. We will not write another book without you.

To Anita Slomski: thanks for your enthusiasm and effort in getting the copy just right. You are a true professional.

To Kate Hawley: thanks for your passion in what you do. We love your style.

To Terry Niego: thanks for your meticulous attention to detail and your brilliant insight.

To the Servant Leaders at Buffini & Company: thanks for your tireless effort to impact and improve the lives of people.

To Niego Real Estate: thanks for your commitment to the Working by Referral system. You are a shining example of its success.

To Steve and Lois Rabey: thanks for your contribution and effort.

To the thousands of Buffini & Company clients: thanks for inspiring us to grow.

Special thanks to our clients and members who have allowed us to use their stories to inspire others.

Table of Contents

The Five Circles of Life

You don't have to be in real estate or lending a long time to realize that your business and life are interconnected. Naturally, your business can have a positive impact on your personal life, such as offering the potential to earn a significant income and the ability to work flexible hours. But our business also tends to be all-consuming, which can quickly rob agents and lenders of any life outside of work.

Each circle in the Buffini & Company logo represents one of the five major areas of a person's life:

> Spiritual
> Family
> Business
> Financial
> Personal (*Physical and Emotional*)

The circles are joined to show that one area of life affects all the others.

Buffini & Company is excited to share with you the Working by Referral system, which takes a holistic approach to operating your business so that all five circles in your life remain linked in harmony.

SECTION I

Embracing the
Relational Approach

CHAPTER ONE

Discovering a Better Way

BY BRIAN BUFFINI AND JOE NIEGO

Two roads diverged in a yellow wood and I . . .
I took the one less traveled by,
And that has made all the difference.

Robert Frost

If you don't know where you are going,
you might end up somewhere else.

Yogi Berra

Discovering a Better Way

We've all seen classic Western movies, many of them starring John Wayne, in which the good guy rides into a dusty town on his faithful horse and becomes the enemy of the bad guys who want to drink, shoot, and generally raise hell.

The good guy relies on his personal code—as well as his handy six-shooter—to fight lawlessness. And to make it easier for us to figure out who's who, the director has the good guy wear a white ten-gallon hat while the bad guys sport big black hats.

For us, this scenario is more than a script for Western movies; it's a mirror of the way things are in the real estate industry. Let us explain.

A Date with Destiny

It was February 10, 1992, and we had both been invited to attend an elite agent conference at the Sir Francis Drake Hotel in downtown San Francisco. Thirty of the most productive agents in real estate were gathering for three days of brainstorming and networking about industry insights and strategies.

Strangers to each other that morning, the two of us were sitting at opposite sides of the room. But a few hours into the conference, we were probably the only two fidgeting in our chairs, uncomfortable with the definitions of success extolled by one super-agent after another. There was a distinct "me-first" attitude among the speakers, who had oversized egos and were a little too slick for our tastes.

Besides inflating their production numbers and gross commissions to outdo each other, these industry giants promoted a customer-service approach best described as "find 'em, fleece 'em, and forget 'em." Clients who were not planning on buying or selling a home within the next 30 days were ignored or, as one agent stated, "I tell them to buy or get out of my car!" And there was nothing fresh or innovative about their sales tactics, which consisted of cold-calling, door-knocking, and other types of *Transactional Approaches*.

As luck would have it though, we sat at the same lunch table where we discovered that we had many things in common. We both came from big families, had played competitive sports, and our business and life philosophies were amazingly in sync. From that day on we've often referred to ourselves as "brothers from different mothers."

For years, both of us had worked exclusively by referral and we could not fathom how the tactics we heard discussed that morning would ever mesh with our beliefs on how to work and how to live. We had built our careers around a philosophy of service that puts the client first. By remaining invested in those relationships for the long haul, we had received the benefit of clients' referrals for years and years to come.

> *At the end of each day, with a cigar wedged between two fingers Harry would point to my work, look me dead in the eye, and ask, "Can you put your name to that today, Brian?"*

We had defined success as a combination of income and the pride we felt in a job well done. Yet many of the speakers that day talked only about money, their material comforts, and industry accolades.

After lunch, the conference attendees were to meet in small groups to discuss their greatest challenges and best ideas. More disappointment: Instead of hearing about great new ideas, we endured four hours of stories about messy divorces, client lawsuits, and petty jealousies.

We also discovered to our chagrin that these people were spending as much as they were making. They were indeed grossing a lot of money, but as we did the math, it became clear that they were spending a considerable amount to generate each lead without keeping much in profit.

We didn't return to the conference the following morning. Instead, we spent the next two days sharing the ideas and concepts that had proven so successful for us, not only in our growing real estate businesses but also in our lives.

Here are the stories of two ambitious young men who wanted to be successful in business but in a way that would allow them to be proud of their profession and build long-lasting relationships with the people they served.

In short, they wanted to be the white hats.

Brian's Story: Stranger in a Foreign Land

I was born and raised in Dublin, Ireland, in a family of five boys and one girl. If you look up "Irish mother" in the dictionary you'll see a picture of my mam! My dad is a fifth-generation painting contractor, and at about the age of 10, I was taught the family trade along with the rest of my brothers.

My grandfather, Harry, oversaw our daily training and instruction as we apprenticed in the trade. At the end of each day, with a cigar wedged between two fingers Harry would point to my work, look me dead in the eye, and ask, "Can you put your name to that today, Brian?" My grandfather was upholding the Buffini tradition of doing work that exceeded customers' expectations so that the company could depend on word-of-mouth advertising. Little did I know that, years later, this same principle would make me a fortune in the real estate business.

The Ireland of my youth was not the economic powerhouse it is today and many ambitious Irishmen beat the well-worn path to the States looking for opportunity. So at the age of 19, with $92 in my wallet and a duffle bag containing all my worldly possessions, I immigrated to America and landed in San Diego, California. I was happy to find any type of work. At various times I sold t-shirts off a cart at Pacific Beach, was a night security guard at the La Jolla Cove Hotel, and developed photos at the local film express.

Then a serendipitous chat with a man in a bar changed my life. Accustomed to the Irish sport of going to a pub to engage in friendly conversation, I had no qualms about chatting with the patron sitting next to me. He told me he was in real estate and handed me a card printed with his name and the words "Million Dollar Club." That got my attention.

After he described his daily activities of selling real estate, he told me, "You'd be great in real estate. You seem like a real people-person," adding that his company provided free training to new recruits.

Two days later I sat nervously in his broker's office, wearing a leather jacket, white shirt and thin gray tie, which was fashionable in Europe at the time, but a little strange for San Diego. As the broker reviewed my hastily assembled resume, I was grateful I had asked my mother to use her direct line to heaven to put in a good word for me.

Mam's prayers were answered. "As soon as you get your license you can start," the broker said. Ninety days later and feeling like I'd just won the lotto, I confidently marched into my new career.

But the training I had banked on was practically nonexistent. So I tried every method I could think of to find clients: cold-calls, door-knocking, direct mail, billboards, even my own real estate radio show. Eventually I moved to the most prestigious realty company in the area and soon became the top agent with closets full of trophies to show for it. In the eyes of my peers, I was a major success.

But I didn't feel successful. After less than two years as an agent and now married with children, I was spending as much in my business as I was making, getting behind on my taxes, and working seven days a week. So many hours were spent trying to generate leads that my clients were getting the leftovers of my time and energy. On the home front, it was common for me to leave before the kids were awake and return home when they were already asleep at night.

I could no longer quell my growing disquiet. The industry was telling me I was a success but I remember thinking, "If I'm successful, what the heck is everyone else doing?"

I went away for a weekend by myself to try to clear the cobwebs. I was seriously thinking of getting out of the business. I reflected on what I had wanted when I first got into real estate, what I had hoped to achieve, and what I wanted my business to do for me and my family.

I thought about my grandfather asking, "Can you put your name to that, Brian?" I thought about past successes in school, especially in sports, and when I compared who I was in my mind's eye to how I was living, the tears of frustration started to flow.

From that moment, I resolved that I would never again care about agent rankings, accolades, or trophies. I realized that my father and grandfather had it right all along. Exceeding my clients' expectations would not only produce the level of income I desired, but I would have a business that would make me proud. I would measure success by how much net income I earned and how well I took care of my clients.

I now had a passion to find a better way to sell real estate, to serve my clients at a deeper level, and have a business that served the needs of my family.

Joe's Story: Breaking the Mold

My seven brothers and sisters and I grew up in a tight-knit, Irish-Catholic blue-collar community on Chicago's South Side. Mom was a homemaker and my father worked for the city of Chicago and also had his own business as a cement finisher. In my neighborhood, you played sports in high school and then got a job with the city as a fireman, police officer, or civil servant. Maybe you went off to college, but you usually came back and *then* went to work for the city.

But I always knew I wanted to break out of the mold. I went to Lewis University, a small liberal-arts college in Romeoville, Illinois, and played basketball. Although I majored in marketing, my dream was to play in the NBA. Figuring that NBA scouts had never heard of my Division II school, I made a highlight video and sent it to every team in the NBA. Despite the zeal with which I pursued my goal, I was still shocked that June day in 1987 when I was selected as the second draft choice of the Houston Rockets.

No NBA team had ever drafted anyone from my neighborhood before and I felt enormous pressure to not let anyone down. I became compulsive in my pursuit of athletic perfection and punished myself daily with the famous Walter Payton workout. I stopped each workout only when I threw up or could no longer bend over to pick up the ball.

To my great surprise, when I arrived at rookie camp and practiced with the Rockets, I found I was in better shape than anyone on the team and my skills were as good or better than those I played against. So why am I in the Real Estate Hall of Fame instead of the Basketball Hall of Fame?

Although my athleticism and game had exceeded the boundaries of my neighborhood, my mind had not. When I practiced with Hakeem "the Dream" Olajuwon, Ralph Samson, and World B. Free—some of the all-time greatest in the NBA—I could hang with them physically, but mentally, I didn't feel I belonged in their league.

I began to notice client patterns and discovered that there was a direct correlation between the quality of the leads I was generating and the sources from which they came.

Doubt crept in. "Who do you think you are?" I would ask myself. "You're just an average Joe from the South Side of Chicago." I had stopped believing in myself, which led to me being released from the team and abandoning my childhood dream.

As I flew home, I felt not only personal loss but also that I'd let down my family and neighborhood. What was I going to do now? Work for the city? I had no idea.

Just a few weeks later, I had a conversation with a man who had grown up in the neighborhood and was a legend for the fortune he had amassed as a real estate investor. On one of his visits back, he told me that the vast majority of millionaires in America owned real estate and that a great way to learn the business was to become a real estate agent. "Don't worry Joe," he told me, "give it 10 years and you'll be making more than any guy in the NBA!"

Before this conversation, the only way I dreamed I could achieve financial success was through professional sports. But now the idea of owning real estate excited and inspired me. With renewed hope, enthusiasm, and a promise to not repeat the mistakes I had made with the NBA, I pursued real estate with passion. As a reminder to never again sell myself short, I created the personal slogan, "Not your average Joe."

Once in real estate, I tried everything and anything to generate business: standing on top of a promotional billboard, dressing up as a leprechaun—admittedly, a very tall one—and handing out cookies to the entire neighborhood, and doling out candy as the Easter Bunny. I tried cold-calling, door-knocking, geographic farming, mass mailings, and every form of advertising. I was working 70 to 80 hours a week and had little to show for it. My intensive basketball workouts seemed like a walk in the park compared to my effort of trying to generate sales.

I will never forget the day I called a "time-out." Becoming very analytical, I rethought every activity I did at work to diagnose the problems in my struggling business. I began to notice client patterns and discovered that there was a direct correlation between the quality of the leads I was generating and the sources from which they came.

The referred leads were more enjoyable, more cooperative, and the most profitable since I didn't have to spend advertising dollars to find them. I also loved the feeling of trust I felt when I met them for the first time and, more than anything, I wanted to do right by them. So I dedicated myself to building my real estate business through referrals and repeat customers.

Now looking back over 2,400 closed transactions, I realize that the time-out I took was the turning point in my career.

The Road to True Success

We believe it was Providence that the two of us met at the conference in San Francisco that day. Since then, we've become strong friends and partnered on many business ventures together. We have brainstormed on how to improve the real estate business almost every day since we've met. And now we travel the world presenting the Working by Referral system we've built to impact and improve the businesses and lives of agents and lenders.

We have faced the same challenges and problems you have faced in your career and we've learned our lessons the hard way. We've struggled with finding a better way to do business, and through trial and error, test marketing, and much evaluation, we believe we've found it.

The good news is these methods create consistency and pre-dictability in both the quality *and* quantity of the leads you'll gener-ate. By using the Working by Referral techniques, we've been able to build businesses that continue to grow and develop. They have revo-lutionized work and life for us and for tens of thousands of people in our industry.

And we'd like to share with you how our principles and practices can dramatically change your career and life as well. Our step-by-step approach will give you the tools to help you become financially suc-cessful and get the most enjoyment out of your work. Join us in learn-ing Working by Referral and prepare to live the good life.

CHAPTER TWO

The Both/And Mindset

BY BRIAN BUFFINI

*Some men see things as they are and say "Why?" I
dream things that never were, and say "Why not?"*
George Bernard Shaw

*Whenever you see a successful business,
someone once made a courageous decision.*
Peter Drucker

The Both/And Mindset

To the casual observer, Collette Horton was on a meteoric path to success. An assistant to an accountant at age 16, Collette was a wholesale mortgage rep by 20 and a broker bringing in a six-figure income by 28.

But as Collette's career grew, her family life withered. Working 70 or more hours a week, she was too spent to play with her five-year-old son, Shawn. And when she went out to dinner with her husband, Terry, she didn't hesitate to take business calls—even during a romantic dinner he arranged for their wedding anniversary. "Talk about not having any boundaries!" says Collette, a broker with Liberty Star Mortgage in Houston.

Collette told herself that it was love for her family that drove her to work brutal hours. But as the couple edged closer to divorce, this explanation no longer made sense. And if you asked Collette what her long-term goals were, she came up blank. "My only goal was to get to the end of the month," she said. "I kept telling myself that I would change things, work fewer hours. But month after month, nothing changed because my business was consuming my life. I had no time for anything or anyone else."

It took a crayon drawing posted on the refrigerator to finally open Collette's eyes. Shawn's teacher had asked him to make a drawing of his family. Shawn had drawn himself, his father, and the family dachshund, Rex. But Collette was AWOL from the picture. Soon after, Shawn's teacher asked Collette during a parent-teacher conference if everything was all right at home, showing her a letter Shawn had written that said, "Dear Mom, When are you coming home? Your friend, Shawn."

"I felt like someone had punched me in the stomach," recalls Collette. "I saw myself as a complete and total failure as a mom and as a wife." When

Collette confided her troubles to a colleague, he said he knew someone who could help. "I signed up for a Business Coach with Buffini & Company the next day," she says.

Collette's Business Coach challenged her to consider the idea that she could continue her successful career and have time and energy for what was really important to her—a happy family. But that meant she would have to be open to a new way of running her business, necessitating both a new mindset and a new way of working.

The Major Breakthrough

Collette didn't intentionally sacrifice her family to her career. But, like many agents and lenders, she gradually drifted into a pattern of work that consumed more and more hours as she rationalized away her dreams of having a balanced, fulfilling life. "Life is what happens to you while you're busy making other plans," sang John Lennon in the song, "Beautiful Boy."

Joe and I speak to thousands of men and women every year who, like Collette, mistakenly think they have to settle for less in their personal lives as they build their businesses. Some are industry veterans like Collette. Others are new agents and lenders who find themselves putting in more and more hours at work, hoping that the time spent will eventually translate into a profitable business.

A month before my nineteenth birthday, as I prepared to leave Ireland and come to America, my father warned me about chasing my financial goals at all costs:

> Son, you've always had a lot of ambition and drive, and America is a place that rewards those character qualities. You'll undoubtedly earn a lot of money and acquire a number of possessions. But I've known many a man who would trade in all his riches to reclaim the time forever lost with his children, the relationship he didn't have with his spouse, or to recapture the years he spent in dogged pursuit of financial success only to discover too late that he'd missed out on many of life's more rewarding experiences.

I didn't doubt the sincerity of my father's advice. But as a 19-year-old, I believed in the infinite opportunities I would find in America. I did not intend to have to choose between having the fullness of life and the financial freedom I desperately wanted. I believed I could achieve both in harmony.

However, as the years passed and my San Diego real estate practice grew, there were too many evenings I came home late for dinner, too many afternoons spent negotiating on a cell phone at my kids' soccer games, and too many hours being preoccupied or giving in to exhaustion when I could have been pursuing my other passions in life.

I was letting my business run my life and I began to wonder whether my father was right all along. Did I have to choose between financial wealth and a happy family life? Did being financially successful mean forfeiting all my other dreams? Could my business only be successful if I spent every waking moment on it? I realized I was in danger of derailing the dreams I had when I first came to America.

My internal conflict between work and family caused me to re-evaluate my life, which also meant taking a hard look at my business. Was there a way to run my business so that I was in control and not at the mercy of unreasonable clients? How could I feel confident engaging in new business opportunities instead of wondering where my next transaction was coming from? Could this seemingly unpredictable business create a predictable income stream with a predictable work schedule? Could I build a business that serves my life, instead of having my life serve my business?

After much reflection and contemplation, I found my answer. Yes, there is a way!

Embracing the Both/And Mindset

We all face similar challenges in balancing our work and personal lives. How can you have *both* a successful career *and* a happy, full life? How can you *both* provide for your family *and* give them the time and love they need? How can you live by your core values *and* be successful in business?

The first step is to simply believe you can. The wealthiest man who ever lived was King Solomon. One of his proverbs states that, "As a man thinketh in his heart, so is he." A person is literally what he thinks, his character being the complete sum of all his thoughts.

We believe that two seemingly opposed desires can indeed exist in harmony if you have a *both/and* mindset. You can have *both* a career and a life, success *and* a loving family, wealth *and* the good life. Think back to the dreams you had when you first went into business for yourself— dreams of being your own boss, working flexible hours, realizing the potential for ever-growing income. You believed your business could be the financial vehicle to fund your life's passions.

Collette went into business for herself for the same reason. But somewhere along the way, she began to see her desire to be a successful broker as being diametrically opposed to being a good mom and wife. That meant she felt forced to choose one and abandon the other—an *either/or* mindset.

Unfortunately, this either/or mindset seems to be prevalent in our industry. We get mired in all the daily details of running a business, losing sight of the desires that first motivated us. Soon *either/or* becomes our default approach and we forget that we had once envisioned more for ourselves. We lose control of our lives and fail to achieve the goals we set when we believed we could have it all.

Some of us try to make up for our frustrations by loading our walls with awards and plaques testifying to our superior production. But no number of shiny brass plaques will ever make up for lost time with a child or abandoning a lifelong dream. We end up chasing the phantom of success instead of the genuine article.

In this book we will be giving you our proven systems for generating high-quality leads and strategies for closing more deals, ultimately leading you to financial success. But if that's all we gave you, we'd

> *"As a man thinketh in his heart, so is he." A person is literally what he thinks, his character being the complete sum of all his thoughts.*
>
> *We believe that two seemingly opposed desires can indeed exist in harmony if you have a* both/and *mindset*

be disappointed because life is so much more than building a business. We want to show you how these systems can offer you both economic success *and* personal happiness.

As Joe and I walk you through our time-tested principles and practices, we want you to think about the dream you had when you first got into this business. Embracing the both/and mindset will enhance your life, making it better and fuller.

From Small Steps to Big Changes

After seven years of Coaching, Collette Horton's life now reflects a both/and philosophy rather than the either/or rut she had gotten herself into.

"When you are the type of mother that your child leaves out of his drawings, the last thing you think you deserve is another child," says Collette. "But thanks to my new both/and philosophy, I made the decision to have another child, a daughter named Tara. I opened an office five minutes from home and I leave work by five o'clock. That may seem like a small thing, but it's huge for me and my family."

Collette is finding more time to do the things that matter most to her. Recently she spent five days volunteering at Pathways, a nonprofit foundation that helps people overcome their barriers to success. "This is a real passion for me," she says. "It's a thrill for me to be able to help people improve their lives by steering them in the right direction and providing affirmation."

Collette's income has continued to grow, not because she is working 70 hours a week but because she is working more effectively and systematically. "I recently met with a local developer who told me, 'We work 24/7 for our clients and we need you to work 24/7, too,' she says. "I told him, 'Then I'm not the lender for you at this time.' Initially the company was shocked by my response and threatened to take its business elsewhere. Now they've come back, respectful of the boundaries I've set around time for my family."

Collette is truly enjoying the best of both worlds—a business that rewards her and a family life that fulfills her.

ACTION STEP

Think of an example of an area in your life
where you've slipped into Either/Or thinking
(*Circle one*)

■ Spiritual

■ Family

■ Business

■ Financial

■ Personal (Physical and Emotional)

CHAPTER THREE

Working by Referral

BY BRIAN BUFFINI

A principle—as its very nature implies—is something which comes first. A principle is a master key which opens a thousand locks; a compass which will guide you, even on an uncharted sea.

E. M. Standing

Drive thy business, or it will drive thee.

Benjamin Franklin

Working by Referral

When Isabel Diaz of Oak Lawn, Illinois, got her real estate license in 1988, she was highly motivated to succeed. Following the path of many agents, she enthusiastically embraced the Transactional Approach of cold-calling, door-knocking, pursuing expired listings, and hosting open houses every weekend. Soon her workweek had expanded to 110 hours.

This hard work seemed to pay off as leads came in and deals were signed. Month after month, Isabel was the top producer in her office and eventually became the top earner in her office for an entire year.

To an outsider, Isabel appeared highly successful. But when I spoke with her, she admitted she wasn't happy. She was spending excessive amounts of money to find leads, she was at the mercy of demanding clients, and she saw no light at the end of the tunnel. She didn't own a business, her business owned her.

"Even though I was working frantically and carrying two cell phones and a pager, I couldn't see my business life getting any better," she told me. "I wondered if I would always work so hard to find a client and then feel the need to prove to them I was valuable. I was exhausted. Even worse, my work life was causing strains in my marriage and distance between me and my children. Plus, I was gaining weight, having health issues, and not feeling good about myself."

To relieve her unhappiness, Isabel shopped. And the worse she felt, the more she bought. Within a couple of years, she was $250,000 in debt, which, of course, pushed her to close more transactions. Living deal to deal, she focused her attention on current clients only and never gave former customers another thought.

After sitting through a Turning Point training seminar, Isabel came up to me. I could tell she'd been crying. Acknowledging her tears, she told me she had finally realized that, "Many of the problems and challenges I face are self-inflicted. But these are also tears of joy because, for the first time, I can see a way out of my situation." Isabel saw that many of the difficulties in her life were symptoms of her business philosophy, which was a Transactional Approach.

Today Isabel is a different person. By systematically applying the techniques and tools of Working by Referral to her business, she is finally experiencing balance in her work, in her life, and in her relationships.

"I am no longer in debt," she said. "I have renewed and restored my relationship with my family. I'm working less and making more, which gives me time to volunteer with organizations I believe in. Now I enjoy the clients I work with. I've managed to achieve a consistent level of income, lost 54 pounds along the way, and I feel great about myself. I love my life!"

Isabel has been so happy with her transformation she has been mentoring other agents since 2005 to show them how they, too, can have both success and balanced lives.

The Light Goes On

My first day in real estate, I was not in a position to help Isabel Diaz or anyone else for that matter. I wasn't even able to help myself. I had joined a small office because I was promised training and I assumed I would get one-on-one attention from the broker.

This did not happen.

My first days were memorable mainly because I felt like the "new kid in school" trying to figure out what to do. I also remember the rapid drain of my bank account as the expenses of my initiation into the business began to add up. The first cell phone I bought was so big it looked as if I was calling in artillery strikes for the army.

The broker brought me into a conference room and gave me three video tapes of a trainer explaining cold-calling, door-knocking, and how to pursue FSBO's and chase after expired listings. After a day and a half of watching videos, I was given a desk, a phone, a list of scripts, and a criss-cross directory.

Picture the scene: I'm an immigrant, I'm broke, and I see real estate as my financial security. I'm willing to do whatever it takes to succeed, but after several days of making calls, I began to think that I was not cut out for this business.

I asked my fellow agents how they coped with making cold-calls. Usually they said, "Oh, I don't do any of that stuff; that's just what they have the rookies do."

"So what do you do?" I asked.

Mostly they talked about walk-ins, sign calls, and floor time. They also told me about the advertising they were doing.

I got the picture that agents were either hard-core prospectors using cold-call techniques, or they sat around waiting for leads to contact them like fishermen sitting on a lake. Problem was, none of these fishermen seemed to have any bait on their hooks.

What I saw didn't jibe with how I thought business should be done. In my past experience with my dad's painting business, all new work came from referrals from former clients and that is how I wanted to work.

> *Every day is a new day in the Transactional Approach; there is no link to the past work you've done or the relationships you've established.*

I now know that the reason the agents in my first office were floundering is because they had fallen into the trap of following the Transactional Approach to business, which unfortunately is still the hallmark of our industry today.

Under the Transactional Approach, agents spend most of their energy finding the next lead. When they get a client, they focus on closing the transaction, getting paid, and then looking for the next lead. They become so preoccupied with finding the next deal, they don't stay in contact with the client they've just served.

It's become the custom in our business to give a client a gift at closing—a bouquet of flowers or basket of fruit—as a token of thanks. But the vast majority of these gifts are actually farewell gifts since the typical agent doesn't ever see that client again.

Every day is a new day in the Transactional Approach; there is no link to the past work you've done or the relationships you've established. I have met 20-year veterans of the real estate business who, every January 1, start from scratch searching for new clients using cold-calling, door-knocking, and advertising. Unfortunately, until they shift their thinking, they will always be one client away from going out of business.

Following the Transactional Approach, I did find a few questionable leads and pursued them with everything I had, even closing some deals. But my business was starting to resemble the old Irish story about a laborer who was assigned to paint a stripe down the center of a country road. The first day he painted a quarter-mile section. The second day he painted only 200 yards. And the next he painted just 50 yards of roadway. "Why has production dropped off so much?" asked his annoyed supervisor.

"It's simple," the laborer said. "The bucket keeps getting further away."

Just like the road painter, I was working too hard with not enough results to show for it. I was basically just a salesperson—a cog in an established system—not the businessman I wanted to be. And the constant stress of worrying where my next deal was going to originate made me as anxious as all the other agents I knew. Depending on personality type, some dealt with the anxiety by working too hard, like I did, while others distracted themselves and played computer solitaire for hours on end, hoping a prospect would call them.

As long as we stuck with this Transactional Approach of doing business, how could we expect anything to change? The answer was we couldn't.

Getting Rid of Relics

Besides being an unproductive and stressful way to work, some of the methods of the Transactional Approach have become obsolete.

In the 1990s, the term "cocooning," coined by the trend-forecaster Faith Popcorn, came into vogue to describe Americans' desire to retreat into their homes and insulate themselves from outside intrusion. Gated communities sprang up, allowing homeowners to control who entered their enclaves. And door-to-door cold-calls became a thing of the past.

Hearing the protests of Americans fed up with being bombarded by telephone sales calls at all hours of the day and evening, the Do-Not-Call Implementation Act of 2003 was signed into law. Similar legislation has already passed in many other countries. Now the old method of picking up the phone book and making cold-calls was also history. Today agents must first consult a Do-Not-Call registry before they pick up the phone. And lenders attempting to contact agents also face an equivalent of the Do-Not-Call law—namely, receptionists who resolutely screen calls and anyone dropping by the office.

Legislative and front-desk firewalls aren't the only obstacles to cold-calling and door-knocking, however. There's also the Golden Rule to consider. After fending off the telemarketing calls, junk mail, and e-mail spam that infiltrate our own homes, many agents don't feel comfortable inflicting similar tactics on others.

Since these traditional methods have become antiquated, one might think the Transactional Approach to acquiring clients has faded over time. Not so. Remember, the Transactional Approach is a philosophy, not a technique. Today, cold-calling and door-knocking have been replaced with pursuing Internet leads, blast e-mail messages, and Web sites as agents continue to search for the next client in a sea of strangers. And, don't forget, once you find a potential buyer or seller using transactional methods, you still have to spend time and energy building the relationship in order to convince your prospect that you offer value and trustworthiness.

Building Relationships that Last

Why do agents continue to use painstaking transactional methods to do business? Many are just trying to survive in a hectic and stressful environment and don't take the time to reflect on and rethink their business strategies. Instead, they just work harder. But working harder isn't the answer; working more effectively and efficiently is.

Fortunately, Do-Not-Call registries, caller ID, and other protective layers of the home cocoon don't have to separate us from potential clients. Working by Referral delivers the highest-quality leads—people who are waiting for your call after getting an endorsement of your character and competence from someone they trust.

Working by Referral is based on agents and lenders maintaining a consistent level of contact with and care for the people in their database (which we'll define later), leading to a steady stream of repeat and referred clients. You'll want to treat these folks with the same care and respect as you would a friend or family member.

There is a widely held belief among agents that you can't expect referrals unless you've been in the business a long time. This is not true. In fact, if you are a new agent or lender, you have an advantage because you haven't been wasting your time using unproductive ways to build your business.

Let's compare the Transactional and Relational Working by Referral attributes.

Transactional Approach	Working by Referral (Relational Approach)
Time-consuming	Time-efficient
Money-intensive	Leverages your investment
Energy-draining	Energy-boosting
Leads to burnout	Relationship-rewarding
Low-quality clients	High-quality, referred clients

The Transactional Approach to business is not only painful in the present, its long-term financial results are bleak, and it eventually creates burnout. New agents may initially get some traction using the Transactional Approach because they have considerable enthusiasm and energy to put behind it. But over time, most agents can't keep up that brutal pace and will want their business to carry them.

The Working by Referral approach produces both a current and future payout. In the present, you will enjoy high-quality leads and a steady income. And with each transaction, you will be building relationships with people who will send you referrals. You will be growing a business instead of making a sale. The production pattern you will experience as illustrated in the graph below is the compounding effect.

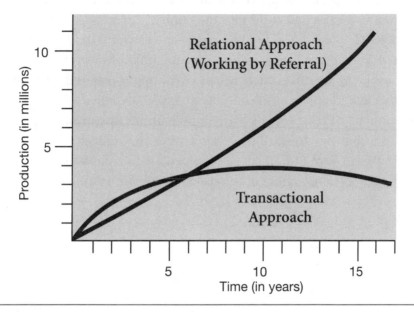

Figure 1. Production Pattern

The Best Payoff

Using the Working by Referral system as the foundation of our real estate businesses, Joe and I have enjoyed the financial rewards of success without sacrificing relationships with family and friends. Time spent at work is productive, and family and personal time is our own.

I was never so grateful for this referral system than when we were expecting our second child. Anthony was then two years old and we were confident we could handle both a toddler *and* an infant. But as Beverly's due date approached, it became harder for me to think about going off to work every day. Anthony was a high-energy boy and I knew how little sleep Beverly would be getting once the baby arrived. And besides wanting to help out, I also wanted to be there to get to know our daughter, Anna.

So I took six weeks off from work to be home with my family. I knew my business would continue to grow even when I was away because this referral system would be generating leads the entire time. I put the cell phone aside, closed the briefcase, and concentrated on welcoming our second child into the family.

When I came back to the office, my assistant had fielded 31 referred leads during my absence. My relational philosophy of doing business had paid off. I officially had a Working by Referral business—one that generated leads even in my absence. My clients were recommending me to their friends and family without my prompting.

From that day forward, no matter what the market conditions, I never worried about finding leads or when I would close my next deal. I will always cherish those six weeks with my family and Working by Referral made them possible.

It can do the same for you.

ACTION STEPS

Evaluate your business.
(*Circle a number*)

I have an abundant flow of incoming leads.
Rarely				Sometimes				Always	
1	2	3	4	5	6	7	8	9	10

I work with high quality leads.
Rarely				Sometimes				Always	
1	2	3	4	5	6	7	8	9	10

I know where my next transaction is coming from.
Rarely				Sometimes				Always	
1	2	3	4	5	6	7	8	9	10

You're in the Lead-Generation Business

BY JOE NIEGO

I need the leads. I need them now. Or I'm gone.
Real estate salesman Shelly Levene
in "Glengarry Glen Ross"

There is only one valid definition of a business enterprise: to create a customer. The customer is the foundation of a business and keeps it in existence.
Peter Drucker

You're in the Lead-Generation Business

"G lengarry Glen Ross" is a great movie—if you can stand watching one gut-wrenching scene after another as the four increasingly desperate salesmen reveal the dark side of the real estate business.

Each of the agents portrayed in the 1992 film knows that quality leads are the key to survival, but not one knows how to generate them. Shelly Levene, played by Jack Lemmon, uses lies and flattery to talk elderly people into signing on the dotted line. Ricky Roma (Al Pacino) buys drinks for a man he meets in a bar, persuading him to buy property that he can't afford and that his wife doesn't want. Meanwhile, the agents played by Alan Arkin and Ed Harris conspire to rob their company of "the good leads" in order to get jobs at a competing agency.

Even Blake (Alec Baldwin), an executive sent to the office to "motivate" the hapless salesmen, can't get them to increase their sales. In his famous "coffee's for closers" monologue, he tells the agents that the one who sells the most properties will get a Cadillac Eldorado. Second prize is a set of steak knives. And third prize? "You're fired," says Blake. "Do I have your attention now?"

Although the dysfunctional real estate office is fictional, the film is dead-on accurate about one thing: This business is all about THE LEADS.

What Business Are You In?

That's the question Brian and I have asked more than a million real estate professionals over the last decade. And the answers, surprisingly, are all over the board: homes, loans, sales, "the people business," and even "the problem-solving business." But in truth, a successful real estate agent is in the *lead-generation* business—an answer we rarely get from audiences.

> *A successful real estate agent is in the lead-generation business.*

And little wonder. According to surveys of Buffini & Company clients, the typical agent spends just 15 percent of his or her time and resources generating leads. That means 85 percent of their time is spent on activities that do not produce leads. This is an imbalance we want to address in this book.

The "Cold" School of Lead-Generation

When I got into the real estate business in 1988, I was eager to learn as much as I could about generating leads. So I signed up for a three-day seminar taught by an ex-Navy Seal who had worked briefly as a real estate agent and thought it was his duty to browbeat the 30 agents attending his seminar—no doubt a style he learned from his drill major during basic training.

The first whiff of trouble came when he marched into the room and locked the door behind him. "What's wrong with you agents?" he bellowed. "I'll tell you what's wrong. You know exactly what to do, but you won't do it!" The implication was clear: We were wimps and afraid of taking action.

He spent an hour teaching us how to make cold-calls. Then he hooked a phone to a speaker in the room and opened a fat phone book. For the rest of the day, we would make cold-calls—one at a time while the other 29 agents listened.

"If you make enough cold-calls, you'll eventually find a lead," he said, which is probably true. But unless you had the steel nerves of a

Navy Seal, you'd also need a big support group to prop you up after the rejection of countless people hanging up on you.

On day two we filed into a Greyhound bus, which took us to a local subdivision so that our drill instructor could teach us the science of door-to-door prospecting. One by one, we were sent out to knock on 15 doors. If we were unlucky enough to find someone at home, a hidden microphone we wore projected our spiel into the bus inching along behind where the rest of the group sat, waiting their turn to pitch a wary homeowner.

I don't know what happened on day three because I didn't go back. But I got his point: Like war, generating leads is hell. And the only thing you can do is grit your teeth and plunge into the fray.

I know hard work is important, but so is working effectively. Methods of searching out strangers didn't ring true with my thoughts on how a successful business should be built. Why should strangers trust me, whom they knew nothing about, with one of their biggest decisions—buying or selling a home? Like Brian, I was convinced there was a better way to find clients, and everything I've learned in the past 20 years has proven this to be true.

Anything *Can* Work but What Works Best?

One day I went to a client's house for an appointment but no one answered the door. Writing a note on the back of my business card requesting that we reschedule, I dropped it in the mail slot and left. As I drove away, I realized I had gone to the wrong house, but it was impossible to retrieve the note. Four months later, I received a phone call from Dean Pepol.

"I've never met you," began Dean, "but you put your business card in my mailbox. My wife and I want to sell our house and buy a condo. Can you help us out?" Within two weeks I had earned $25,000 in commissions from my new client.

So although aimlessly scattering your business cards around can work, any clients you capture with this technique will be a fluke. You can probably dream up dozens of other methods to attract potential clients. I once climbed to the top of a company billboard advertisement 50 feet high for promotional pictures in order to drum up new business. It was certainly an adventure, but not a profitable one.

The point is, any method of generating leads will work. Some methods will require substantial time and will be labor-intensive (open houses, floor time). Some will require a considerable outlay of money (newspaper ads, promotional pieces, random mailings). Some methods will be energy-zapping (pursuing expired listings and FSBOs). All will produce some leads.

But is there a way of generating a lead that is less time-consuming, less costly, more rewarding, and actually enjoyable?

There is!

Not All Leads Are Created Equal

Up to this point, we have assumed that all leads are created equal. But if you have been in the real estate business for more than 30 days, you'll know this is definitely not true.

> *Not all leads*
>
> *are created equal.*

Most of us have tried generating leads by holding an open house or taking floor time.

If you think back, you'll realize that most of the contacts you spoke to didn't buy or sell a home with you. And the few that resulted in a transaction tended to be more demanding, uncooperative, and very price conscious because they were leery of doing business with someone they didn't know.

In contrast, I'm hoping you've also had the opportunity to work with clients who were referred to you, maybe from a family member or friend. Chances are, these people were a pleasure to work with because they trusted you. They were serious about buying or selling their home, were loyal to you, and were happy to pay you for the value you brought.

I experienced this difference in the quality of leads early in my career. During my first-ever open house, I met a man who was enthusiastic about buying a home in the area. After a 20-minute conversation, he gave me his name and phone number and agreed to work exclusively with me to find a house. But I discovered that the number he gave me was for someone else's fax machine. Obviously he had no intention of working with me. He was a lead, but a very low-quality one.

In contrast, Jim G. was referred to me by his friend, who happened to be one of my former high-school instructors. I showed Jim numerous homes, none of which fit his criteria. One Sunday, Jim was driving in an area outside the neighborhoods he had been considering and saw a sign for an open house. Before entering the home, Jim instructed the agent, "I'm currently working with Joe Niego of Niego Real Estate. I would like to see this home but will view it now only if you'll allow Joe to represent me if I decide to purchase it. If not, I am happy to view the home another day accompanied by Joe."

I only learned of this conversation because the agent at the open house called me on Monday looking for feedback. She sheepishly relayed that she had tried to persuade Jim to work with her, but he had remained resolute that he would work only with me. "I wish my clients were as fiercely loyal," the agent commented.

We all need leads, but what type of lead do you really want? You can opt for a "cold" low-quality lead that takes time, money, and energy to find and turns into a challenging client. Or would you rather have a "warm" high-quality lead referred from someone you know and who becomes an enjoyable, loyal client? If it's the latter, then Working by Referral can deliver those leads in spades.

ACTION STEP

Remember the top three activities you need to do every day are:

1. Lead-Generation
2. Lead-Generation
3. Lead-Generation

SECTION II

Getting Down
to Business

CHAPTER FIVE

Discovering the Riches Beneath Your Feet

By Joe Niego

Opportunity is missed by most people because it is dressed in overalls and looks like work.

Thomas Edison

You are, at this moment, standing right in the middle of your own "acres of diamonds".

Earl Nightingale

Discovering the Riches Beneath Your Feet

Folklore tells the story of an Oklahoma rancher named George Jones whose raw ambition to be successful blinded him to the wealth he already had. George's father was one of the original Oklahoma "Sooners" who had acquired extensive land holdings and ranches. George inherited his father's land but was not content working it. The labor was hard and George couldn't see how dirt would ever make him wealthy.

Then around 1849 George heard about a once-in-a-lifetime opportunity. Gold fever had come to northern California and George was entranced by tales of men making fabulous fortunes overnight. The way George saw it, getting rich was simply a matter of having enough pluck to leave Oklahoma for the sun-splashed hills of California. He hurriedly sold his ranch lands for 50 cents on the dollar, packed up his family, and moved to gold country in 1850.

No one's sure what happened to George after that. Some say he invested in a series of unsuccessful mining ventures. Others say he opened a hardware store in San Francisco. But one thing's for sure: George never became one of the fortunate few who struck it rich.

Meanwhile, back in Oklahoma, a gold rush of another kind was bubbling under the soil. In the early 1900s, wildcatters discovered oil throughout Oklahoma. One of the largest oil strikes took place on the land that George had sold so cheaply. If only George had known that all the riches and fortune he hungered for had been right there beneath his feet.

I tell this story because it mirrors what I often see in the real estate industry. I've met many ambitious, driven agents who, in their rush to make money fast, succumb to the latest sales fads, such as buying lists of "guaranteed leads," or attempt to build business the "easy" way with four-color brochures and advertising.

These same agents have lost sight of their core business—generating high-quality leads from the people they already know—and are blind to the potential riches waiting to be mined right in their own backyards. All they need is a disciplined and systematic way to tap that vein of gold, which will deliver the steady stream of high-quality referrals that will make them successful.

Looking Beyond the Next Deal

Recently I took a video camera to the streets of Chicago to interview ordinary people on their views of the real estate industry. Walking up to strangers, I asked, "Do you remember the name of your real estate agent?" The answer was typically No. "I know what she looks like, but I don't remember her name," said one woman. Another said, "I would have to look it up."

And the reason most people drew a blank: Their agent hadn't bothered to maintain contact after the purchase or sale of the home.

> *Whether you're an agent or a lender, there's tremendous pressure to focus on the next deal and the deal after that without devoting time and attention to the long-term growth of your business..*

Whether you're an agent or a lender, there's tremendous pressure to focus on the next deal and the deal after that without devoting time and attention to the long-term growth of your business. That's generally the case whether you've been in the business for one year or 20. One veteran agent told me, "Each day I feel as if I'm starting all over again to get to the next deal. I have no sense of making any long-term gains and of actually building a business."

Our Working by Referral system capitalizes on generating leads from your existing contacts, including former clients, so you don't have to reinvent your business anew each day. But in order to have your name at the forefront of people's minds when they're thinking about buying or selling a house, you need to develop the primary tool of Working by Referral: a database.

From Names to Relationships

A database is not simply a list of names, phone numbers, and addresses; that's a personal phone book. Rather, a database is a list of relationships. If you're a new agent, you may think a database will take years to create. But you'll see that you can generate a working database in an hour. Veteran agents may assume they already have a database. But if

> *A database is a list of relationships.*

you haven't been intentional and strategic about developing and maintaining that database, all you really have is a list of past deals.

For more than 20 years, Bill Stewart of Novato, California, rarely contacted former clients after he closed deals. Before attending the Turning Point, his real estate business stalled at $3.5 million in annual sales.

"I'm not flashy or pushy," says Bill. "I took a passive approach based on word of mouth because I didn't think I could do anything to create referrals." When Bill's wife, Nancy, decided to leave her nursing career to join him in real estate, the pressure became more intense on their business. After a brief and unsuccessful period of door-knocking, Nancy worried that she had made a mistake leaving nursing.

But after working with a Buffini & Company Business Coach, the Stewarts started a database, which included their many business contacts in their community. Now the painters and handymen Bill and Nancy refer clients to also refer their customers to the Stewarts. The couple stays in contact with everyone in their database monthly. Within seven years of Working by Referral and building their database, they closed over $40 million a year in sales.

"After learning how to apply a system to my database, our referrals increased consistently as well as the quality of our clients," says Bill. "I'm enjoying the business more than I ever have. I feel renewed."

Going for the Gold

When new agents join our office, I challenge them to make a list of all the people they know. Typically, they'll spend 30 minutes compiling a list of 20 names. "Good," I say. "Now think of 20 more."

In another 45 minutes, their list is longer. I prompt them to add another 20 names to it, reminding them not to forget the owner of the dry cleaner they see every other Saturday or the mechanic who fixes their car.

When I first put together my own database in 1988, I distinctly remember compiling a list with 86 names on it. Making that list was like throwing a rock into a pond and watching the ripples spread out as one name led to another.

> *The best leads will come from people with whom you have a relationship.*

So if a database of 100 names is good, aren't 1,000 names even better? Not necessarily. You don't strike oil by digging a mile wide and an inch deep; you've got to dig deep. The goal is not to have the biggest database but to have one that delivers results. And the best leads will come from people with whom you have a relationship.

Here are places to start building your database:

- **Friends and family**
  Transfer your holiday-card list directly to your database.

- **Current clients**
  Can you remember the last time you bought a car? If you were like me, you probably found yourself noticing the cars other people were driving just before and after you made your purchase. That's because our brain filters all the millions of pieces of data we process every day in search of the data that really matter.

When a person is engaged in buying or selling a home, they have a heightened awareness of others going through the same process. They naturally gravitate toward comparing real estate notes with those they know who are also buying or selling. I have discovered that current clients are an often-overlooked source of referrals.

- **Past clients**

  Eighty-two percent of people who had sold a home report that they would definitely or probably use the same agent the next time they sell, according to the National Association of Realtors' *2006 Profile of Home Buyers & Sellers*. That means you shouldn't give your past clients the chance to forget your name, as all those Chicagoans I'd polled on the street had done. Don't worry if you haven't made contact with former clients for years. There are simple and effective ways to reconnect with previous clients, who are usually happy to hear from their agent again. (We discuss how in Chapter 7.)

- **Groups and associations**

  Are you a member of a sport or bridge club, a hobby group, the PTA, or a religious organization? I coach my son's fifth-grade basketball team and attend my other son's baseball games. As I get acquainted with the parents of my sons' teammates, I add them to my database when it's appropriate.

- **Business associates and networks**

  Networking through your local chamber of commerce or national groups like Business Network International is a great opportunity to add names to your database. I've also expanded my database with the names of service providers that I draw upon when clients ask for referrals to other professionals, such as electricians, roofers, attorneys, title representatives, carpet retailers and installers. As I refer my clients to them, I actively request referrals in return.

A hard-working database

In 1994, I put the referral system and my database to the test when I went on vacation with my sister, Terry. We were both single at the time and needed a break. Terry took control of planning the trip and I was stunned when she announced that we were going to Australia—*for five weeks*. When I protested that I couldn't possibly be away from the office that long, she said, "Too late, the trip's booked."

So we went, had a great time, and when we returned I had 37 referred leads waiting for me like the morning newspaper on the doorstep. Most of those leads turned into transactions.

If you're stuck in a production rut or feel like you're banging your head against an income ceiling, it's time to try a different approach. Whether you're a new agent or a veteran, it's never too late—or too soon—for you to change how you do business.

ACTION STEPS

■ Use the direction in this chapter to identify 100 relationships for your database.

■ Your goal is to compile 100 names within the next 100 days. If you need a memory jogger, go to www.buffiniandcompany.com and download Hidden Sources of Wealth.

■ If you already have a database (minimum 100), double check to make sure you have the proper address and phone number for each relationship.

CHAPTER SIX

Sorting and Qualifying Your Database

By Brian Buffini

*Standing in the middle of the road is very dangerous;
you get knocked down by traffic from both sides.*

Margaret Thatcher

*When you have to make a choice and you don't make it,
that itself is a choice.*

William James

Sorting and Qualifying Your Database

L ike any cat, the mighty lion can chase down, capture, and eat a mouse. As a snack or appetizer, a mouse may offer a pleasant diversion for the king of the jungle. But if mice are all he prefers or can get, the lion will starve as he expends energy to pursue prey that won't sustain him.

Similarly, agents can find plenty of opportunities to chase after potential clients who will consume their time and energy. But like the lion subsisting on mice while dreaming of antelope, your business and your dreams of success will wither as you waste your resources pursuing clients who never close deals. In this chapter, I will give you a strategy that will allow you to be more efficient and effective when working with clients.

Making the Grade

All people are created equal, but all potential clients are not. Lest you think me judgmental or harsh, let me explain that I'm not talking about a client's worth as a human being. Rather, I'm referring to differentiating between customers who represent future value to your business and those who don't.

Everyone has to use his or her resources of time, energy, and money wisely. And agents and lenders have to focus their resources on those individuals who are likely to use them in future real estate transactions or who will refer others to them.

Other effective businesses also offer special considerations to preferred customers. Take the airline industry, for example. My first few years of presenting training seminars, I flew on many different airlines. Some airlines recognized my repeat business and rewarded me with perks, such as an upgraded seat or coupon to use their private clubs at airports. The greater the rewards from a particular airline, the more I was inclined to travel with it. And when one airline labeled me an A$^+$ passenger, I became a loyal customer, spending over \$240,000 a year on all our staff's flights.

As a young real estate agent, I would work with anyone who could fog a mirror and showed an interest in buying or selling a home. I was willing to do anything my customers asked, provided it wasn't illegal, in hopes that my extra effort would lead to a closing. "Barry" was one such client. Although it was evident from the start that he was unreasonable and demanding, I showed him 46 homes. In the end, all I got for my hard labor was a lack of respect for my profession and me.

> I've found that the Pareto Principle also rings true in the Working by Referral system: 20 percent of the people in your database will generate 80 percent of your referrals.

I quickly learned that people like Barry would drain my time and energy and distract me from finding clients who would close deals. At about the same time, I discovered the Pareto Principle, named after the Italian economist Vilfredo Pareto who observed that 20 percent of the people in Italy owned 80 percent of the country's wealth. Pareto's so-called "80-20 rule" came to be applied to business, creating such accepted maxims as, 80 percent of sales are generated by 20 percent of clients. I've found that the Pareto Principle also rings true in the Working by Referral system: 20 percent of the people in your database will generate 80 percent of your referrals. Joe and the thousands of agents and lenders we coach have also found this to be the case in their businesses.

Of course this isn't a hard-and-fast rule, but it illustrates the importance of ranking the names in your database with the grades A, B, C, or

D so you are spending your resources where the payoff is the greatest. Buffini & Company research has found that 40 percent of agents' and lenders' referrals come from A$^+$ clients. Maintaining relationships with your A$^+$ list is not only good for business, it's also fun to spend time around people who recognize your value!

But remember that a database is not a mailing list. You should have a relationship with everyone in your database and they should recognize your name instantly when you call.

Now it's time to sort your database by the quality of each relationship. I've found that in business as well as life, the closer the relationship, the more time you want to spend with that person. Those at the top of your database will be the people to whom you give your greatest attention. Here's how to categorize the names in your database:

> *You should have a relationship with everyone in your database and they should recognize your name instantly when you call.*

The people who send you multiple referrals: A$^+$
These folks are your ravin' advocates. They love you and think they are doing people a favor by referring them to you. Most A$^+$ names will be past or present clients who have experienced your exemplary service and skill firsthand.

People most likely to refer to you: A
Past clients with whom you have a good relationship belong in the "A" category. They haven't made multiple referrals to you yet, but it's just a matter of time before they do and move up to an "A$^+$" rank. Family members and good friends also belong here.

People who would refer to you if asked and shown how: B
Neighbors or acquaintances with whom you share a common interest—your children and their children are classmates, they are members of your church, you see them at your garden club meetings—should be ranked with a "B." They may not yet know that you are in

real estate, so as you build relationships with them, tell them you're an agent and would be happy to have their referrals.

People who might refer to you in the future: C

"C" people are in the infancy stage of a relationship with you. You feel that you click with them and are hoping to get to know them better.

People to be deleted from your database: D

These are people who are demanding and difficult. It takes energy to be around them and when you see their names on caller ID, you don't pick up the phone.

Deleting these names from your database is empowering—even if you're desperate for business. As crazy as it sounds, go ahead and do it. No matter how much time and energy you spend with these people, they aren't going to close deals or send you referrals. So with their names gone from your database, you've gained more freedom to focus on people who will be beneficial to your business and help you prosper.

Whenever I pruned my database of "D" people, I bid them farewell by mimicking the way my son Alex said goodbye when he was younger. To ensure that everyone in the room paid attention to him when he departed, Alex would give a big smile, wave, and say with flair, "bye-bye now!" With the same fanfare I'd dispatch my "D" list and it felt great.

Putting an "A" List to Work

Sam and Edith Elzie of Bear, Delaware, came to our Turning Point™ training seminar in 1996. Like many agents, they had a long list of people they knew—440 names to be exact. But the list was just a disorganized compilation of names, not a true database. And it was obvious the couple wasn't using it to generate leads; they had done only 13 transactions the previous year.

Sam and Edith joined our ClubNet Coaching program that day and began to work with Coach Roibin McFarling to sort and qualify their list. They pared their list of 440 names to 42 "A" clients. During the next 12 months, the couple's database generated 308 referrals, resulting in almost 100 qualified leads. After sending out their first Client Appreciation Program™

mailing (the Items of Value we develop every month discussed in Chapter 9,)
they closed 12 referrals in 90 days.

Today their database consistently produces as many as 26 quality refer-
rals every month. Sam and Edith have also taught our Working by Referral
system to agents across the country as well as to members of their team.

Now It's Your Turn

Take enough time to really think about the people in your database
before you assign them a letter. Remember, you are not grading people on how much you like or dislike them. You are just determining
who will best be able to generate the referrals that will make your
business grow.

You now have your database and need to turn it into a tool that
will help you generate that steady stream of referrals that is key to our
business model for success. We suggest you use a simple contact man-
agement computer software like ACT! by Sage to group the names in
your database according to the A$^+$ through D designations.

ACTION STEP

Use the criteria in this Chapter to assign a value to the relationships
you identified in Chapter 5. If you find yourself unsure about what
value (A, B, C, and D) to assign a relationship, give the benefit of the
doubt with a higher value and adjust over time. This action step will
take 30 minutes to sort and qualify 100 names.

Engaging Your Database

BY JOE NIEGO

Don't judge each day by the harvest you reap,
but by the seeds you plant.
Robert Louis Stevenson

Whatever you can do, or dream you can, begin it.
Boldness has genius, power and magic in it.
Goethe

CHAPTER SEVEN

Engaging
Your Database

I f you've ever flown into Chicago's Midway Airport, you've probably passed over the very first home I owned in the melting-pot
neighborhood of West Lawn Park. Also home to the tall Native-
American statue seen in the movie "Wayne's World," West Lawn Park
consists of compact three-bedroom homes with lawns the size of
postage stamps.

I lived next door to a retired steelworker named Henry who nur-
tured and manicured his tiny plot of grass with all the love and care of
the head greens keeper at Augusta National Golf Club.

In contrast, my lawn looked more like an abandoned cow pasture.
With the pride of new home ownership and a desire to "keep up with
the Joneses," I started asking neighbors how I could turn my mess of
a yard into a beautiful, lush lawn overnight.

"You can't," admonished an elderly Polish woman who lived
down the street. "It takes time."

I started spending evenings and weekends raking, seeding, water-
ing, and fertilizing. Two months later, I knew I had succeeded when
Henry walked over and said, "Hey, Joe, your lawn is giving mine some
stiff competition."

My lawn did look great but it took a lot of care and attention. The
same is true of client databases, which are not unlike living organisms.
If you neglect a database, it will wither and become dormant, failing
to provide you with the leads you need to grow your business. But if
you cultivate the relationships within your database, they will reward
you with referrals. In this chapter, I'm going to give you the tools to
nurture your database and make it work for you.

Words Are the Water

Like a growing lawn, your database needs the right combination of elements to flourish. New names are the seeds you add to your database. With proper care, many will become A and A⁺ clients. Your D clients are like crabgrass; get rid of them quickly to make room for people who are happy to refer you to others.

> *Like a growing lawn, your database needs the right combination of elements to flourish.*

Words are like water, sustaining our relationships with clients, past and present. Real estate agents constantly traffic in communication. But we are not always as careful as we should be with our words, even though they leave indelible impressions. People continually evaluate our words for clues about our character, motivation, and concerns.

> *People continually evaluate our words for clues about our character, motivation, and concerns.*

You can, however, be more intentional about the words you use—and the impact they have on clients—by using the tools we call Dialogs and Letters.

The Mayor Campaign Dialog

This is a simple Dialog you can use to turn a casual conversation with someone you meet at a party or ball game into a potential relationship to add to your database. We call it the Mayor Campaign because agents and lenders are always reaching out to people and asking them to elect to work with them when they buy or sell—not unlike a mayoral candidate campaigning for votes.

Weave the Mayor Campaign Dialog into your conversation naturally:

"If you were buying or selling a home, or had a friend or family member who was, do you have an agent you'd refer them to?"

If their response is Yes, that's OK; just continue your conversation. If they reply No, say:

"Well, I'd like to be that person for you. From time-to-time I come across valuable real estate information that everyone finds helpful. Would you like to receive that?"

Now the majority of people will say Yes, so follow up with:

"Great! So where's the best place for me to send this information?"

Once they've given you a street address, your next goal is to get their phone number:

"If I needed to get in touch with you, what's the best number to reach you?"

Then hand them your business card and say:

"I'm going to stay in contact with you and if you know anyone who is thinking about buying or selling a home, just give me a call with their name and business number and I'll be happy to follow up and take great care of them."

You now have a new relationship—attached to a name, address, and phone number—to add to your database. You don't yet know whether this person will be a good source of referrals, so for now categorize him or her as a "C" client.

Adding new names through the Mayor Campaign Dialog is how you keep your database fresh and growing. Of course, you have to continually sort your database, pushing names to the top as they send you referrals and pruning those who never do.

Introduction Letter

If you are new to the business or are just starting to build a database, don't assume that everyone knows you sell real estate and that you would be happy to receive referrals. You have to let them know. The

Dear Adam,

The reason for this letter is to inform you of my Client Appreciation Program. Every month I send our valuable tips and information to a select group of people. You will receive information on topics such as home budgeting, health and fitness, or remodeling your home in addition to valuable real estate information.

I make a constant effort to improve the level of service I provide to you because, in my business, the most profound assets I possess are your respect and trust.

I'll contact you soon to see if I can be of any help or meet any of your needs.

Yours sincerely,

Amy Girlson

Oh, by the way..., if you know of someone thinking of buying or selling a home, who would appreciate the kind of service I offer, I'd love to help them. So, as these people come to mind, just give me a call with their name and business number. I'll be happy to follow up and tend to their needs.

Figure 2. Introduction Letter

Introduction Letter communicates that you value the relationship and would welcome the opportunity to help with any real estate needs. It also informs recipients that you'll be sending them valuable real estate and lifestyle information (discussed in Chapter 9) and that you will be following up with a phone call (see Figure 2 on page 62).

Confession Letter

During our presentations, Brian and I ask audience participants to raise their hands if they have *not* been in contact with previous clients—either face to face or by telephone—since the day of their closing. Hundreds of hands go up. And when we ask participants to keep their hands up if they would like to reconnect with those clients, very few hands come down.

As the old saying goes, "Confession is good for the soul," and in this case it's also good for re-establishing contact and a relationship with former clients. The Confession Letter offers your apologies for not staying in touch and affirms how much you value former clients and would be honored to work with them again. And like the Introduction Letter, it also states that you'll be sending them important information through your complimentary Client Appreciation Program and that you'll be calling them (see Figure 3 on page 64).

The "Big Three" Dialog

Now that you've sent a letter to everyone in your database, it's time to call them. Many agents are apprehensive about the follow-up phone call because they don't know what to say. But by using the following Big Three Dialog as a guide, your call will sound natural and will impart three key messages.

Can I be of any help?
Communicate your willingness to be of assistance to your contacts, whether they are long-term clients or people with whom you've never done business.

HI, IT'S ME!

Dear Alysha,

Working with you in the past was really enjoyable for me, and I'm glad I could be of service. Since then, I must admit that I haven't stayed in as close contact with you as I would have liked. I now understand that the kind of people I want to work with in the future are great people just like you.

Let me take just a moment of your time to let you know about my **Client Appreciation Program**. I am making constant effort to improve the level of service I provide to my clients. Every month I will be sending out valuable tips and information that I hope you will find useful.

This month's **Item of Value** is on the topic of home improvement and includes a list of the top **Businesses I Refer**. These are service providers that I trust to give all my family, friends and clients excellent service. Please feel free to call on them whenever you have a need they might be able to meet.

My goal is to build out a more comprehensive **Business Directory** online which will include trades and services my clients have had great experiences with. You'll be hearing more about this in a later email.

I look forward to talking with you soon.

Yours sincerely,

Grant George

Oh, by the way . . ., if you know someone thinking of buying or selling a home, who would appreciate the service I offer, I'd love to help them. So, just give me a call with their name and business number and I'll be happy to follow up and take excellent care of them.

Figure 3. Confession letter

"Hi, Connor. This is Alex calling. How are you doing? How's the family?

The reason I'm calling is because I want to know if you received the information I sent you on how to prevent identity theft. I hope you found it helpful.

Also keep in mind that if you need a referral for a painter, a plumber, or some other service, let me know because I come across some good tradespeople in my work."

The value you represent to me

Let your contacts know you value them.

"Connor, I want to make sure you know how much I value our relationship. I want to build my business by working with people like you."

Oh, by the way® . . .

This message is vitally important. As you conclude the phone call, give a reminder that you are looking for people who are thinking of buying or selling a home.

"Oh, by the way . . . Connor. If you know someone who wants to buy or sell a home, I'd love to help them. Just give me a call with their name and business number and I'll be happy to follow up and take great care of them. I'm never too busy for any of your referrals."

We owe the inspiration for this message to Columbo, the badly dressed and seemingly inept TV police detective played by Peter Falk. Often just as Columbo was about to leave the room, he would raise his hand in the air, hold it to his forehead, and say to his prime suspect, "Oh, by the way . . . " That nonthreatening phrase lowered the defenses of the suspects Columbo was interviewing and gave him access to the secrets they were guarding.

When you say, "Oh, by the way . . ." as if it were an afterthought, you're gently priming the person for your key marketing message. You can now ask for referrals in a direct way without being overbearing.

In asking for a contact's referrals, you are also asking for his or her trust. We want our clients to know that we value and appreciate this demonstration of trust and that we will honor it by taking great care of the people they refer by exceeding their expectations. You want to convey that you are passionate about what you do, you do your job well, and by expanding your network, you can help even more people. Your goal is for referred clients to thank their friends for making the introduction to you.

The Big Three Dialog is a direct way to communicate that you want to help, that you value your relationships with people, and that you're never to busy to receive referrals. If you master this Dialog, you'll be building your business with everyone you contact.

The New Agent Dialog

If you haven't been in business long, you can transform your lack of experience from a liability to an asset with this Dialog. When someone warily asks how long you've been in real estate, answer this way:

"I'm newer to the business but I have a lot of energy. I'm fired up, I'm enthusiastic, and I have time to help you. If we encounter a problem that I don't know the answer to, I'm one phone call away from people in my office who have many years of experience. I'll get you the answers you need."

The Fruits of Your Labors

When I began cultivating my database, I added Tom B., who is the father of a high-school classmate of mine. Tom was then 54 and had rented a home his entire life. Although many people would call Tom a poor prospect for real estate, I sent him my Introduction Letter and followed up with regular phone calls.

One day when I called Tom he made a startling announcement. "You know, Joe," he said, "I've been thinking about what you've been telling me about home ownership and I am ready to make a change. Can you find me a house?"

We quickly found a wonderful property at a good price. Tom was thrilled, which made me happy, too. And his enthusiasm for home ownership was contagious. In short order, he began to call with new clients for me.

"I have eight children and I don't want them renting their entire lives like me," Tom said. "I had a really good experience working with you. Can you help some of my kids find homes, too?"

Over the next six months I helped four of Tom's children find homes. And Tom's kids referred me to other clients, who referred me to even more clients.

Our industry is full of frustrated people who seek short-term fixes. But there's no quick way to build a client database. Instead, you need to nurture and cultivate it day by day. The results, however, are well worth the commitment.

ACTION STEPS

Newer Agent:

- ◼ Memorize the New Agent Dialog and look for an opportunity to use it within the next seven days.

- ◼ Memorize the The Big Three Dialog and the Mayor Campaign.

- ◼ Download a copy of the Introduction Letter from www.buffiniandcompany.com and send it to all the names in your database.

Seasoned Agent:

- ◼ Memorize the The Big Three Dialog and The Mayor Campaign and use them ten times within the next seven days.

- ◼ Identify the past clients you have not been in contact with in the last 12 months.

- ◼ Download a copy of the Confession Letter from www.buffiniandcompany.com and send it to each of those clients.

CHAPTER EIGHT

The Three C's to Success

BY BRIAN BUFFINI

It is not your customer's job to remember you. It is your obligation and responsibility to make sure they don't have the chance to forget you.

Patricia Fripp

The secret to success is constancy of purpose.

Benjamin Disraeli

The Three C's
to Success

When I was growing up in the old sod, my mam used to make an Irish stew that brought all us kids running to the dinner table. Now Irish stew is ordinarily no gourmet dish. But mam had a secret; she slipped in a mixture of herbs and spices that transformed the stew of lamb, potatoes, and onions into a sheer taste delight. Friends and family would often ask for her recipe and she would oblige—conveniently forgetting to mention at least one herb or spice. No sense in turning a secret recipe into a common commodity was Mam's attitude.

Buffini & Company also has a special recipe for real estate and lending professionals called the Three C's to Success. But, unlike mam's carefully guarded recipe, we're happy to share all the ingredients with you.

The Three C's stand for Contact, Care, and Community, and blending them into your business systems will generate high-quality referrals. It's crucial that you apply all three elements, however. Neglecting even one of the Three C's destroys the powerful synergy you get when all three are working together. We like to say that this compounding effect on your database is like adding 1 + 1 and getting 11 instead of 2. While this may not seem obvious to you at first, you'll see what we mean when the results begin to show.

> *The Three C's stand for Contact, Care, and Community, and blending them into your business systems will generate high-quality referrals.*

In the next three chapters we'll give you all the details you need to successfully put the Three C's in play and enjoy a quality of life that may have eluded you in the past. To give you a taste, however, here's a brief overview.

Contact

Regular contact with the people in your database keeps your name top-of-mind so they'll automatically think of you when they need an agent or lender. In Chapter 9, we'll show you specific ways to contact people in your database to deepen your relationship with them. Carefully worded scripts can take the dread out of making follow-up phone calls, and our Client Appreciation Program (CAP) will entice people to read the mail they receive from you instead of throwing it in the trash unopened.

Care

Rhetoric about the exemplary care people will receive when they become customers is standard in many businesses. Sometimes those words become reality but, too often, actions don't live up to promises.

In Chapter 10 you'll find out how to earn customers' trust that you'll truly care for them in any real estate or lending dealings. For example, writing personal notes to some of the people in your database every working day can demonstrate your care. Another technique is the Pop-By, where you visit a person's home for a very brief visit and drop off a little token gift that the individual will appreciate receiving.

Community

Developing a sense of community with people in your database enhances the care you give and provides meaningful connections with you and others. We use client parties and business lunches to build community in a world where technology can isolate us and take the joy of personal relationships out of business transactions. In Chapter 11, you'll read about ways that agents and lenders have created environments for interactions that not only generate life-long clients but also enrich relationships.

The Recipe Frees Up Time

Right now you may be wondering how the Three C's will lead to greater freedom in your life when you have to make time to write notes, make personal visits, and host parties. The good news is that once you establish the Three C's as part of your business system, nurturing the people in your database will take much less time than starting over every day trying to drum up new business.

Mam never watched the pot of stew simmer all day; she simply put the ingredients together, gave them a stir now and then, and got great results. It's the same with the Three C's. It takes only minutes a day to write a few notes and make calls, and you can map out a route to do Pop-Bys on the way home from work. And since most of us take time out of our day to eat lunch, why not occasionally invite people from your database to join you?

Unlike the many hours you now spend hunting for leads that may not go anywhere, the time you spend incorporating the Three C's into your business is manageable and under your control. The key, however, is to apply all three elements consistently. Once the Three C's become a routine part of the way you do business, the people who are the recipients of your contact, care, and community will be generating quality leads for you while you are working with your current clients. And, suddenly, you'll be working efficiently as your business continues to grow as you are living your life.

> *Once the Three C's become a routine part of the way you do business, the people who are the recipients of your contact, care, and community will be generating quality leads for you while you are working with your current clients.*

Remember, contact without care is transactional. Care without contact will not produce leads. And contact and care need the element of community to generate repeat and referred business. These are the ingredients for a great business.

73

Creating Value Through Trust

When trying to secure a listing or buyer, most salespeople make the mistake of first attempting to get the potential client to like them. But just because you exude friendliness doesn't mean people are going to do business with you or refer you. What criteria do homeowners or prospective buyers use to hire an agent? How do people differentiate among agents?

To answer these questions, you first have to understand how consumers make purchasing decisions. Every consumer will weigh value and benefit against the cost of the goods or service. If the value and benefit are greater than the cost, a consumer will buy. If the value and benefit are less than the cost, they won't buy. And when consumers cannot recognize a measurable difference in value and benefit between options, they will make their purchasing decision strictly on price. It's little wonder, then, that agents with no way to display value to their clients are constantly tempted to lower their commissions in order to compete.

> *To differentiate yourself from the competition, you must communicate your value.*

To differentiate yourself from the competition, you must communicate your value. We think the best way to do that is to establish trust with your clients through the Three C's.

Business trust is built on both character and competence. Character is what we typically associate with trust, using terms such as integrity or "our word is our bond." But competence also plays a role in building trust. People hold professionalism, consistency, communication, and technical knowledge in high regard.

As you read about the ways to demonstrate contact, care and community in the rest of this book, you'll see many examples of how Working by Referral can communicate competence *and* character. And that's important because the ultimate goal of this Relational Approach is for people to trust you not only with their business but to also be willing to endorse you to their friends and family.

During our many years in real estate together, Joe and I have shared numerous stories of clients and real estate dealings with each other. Joe once told me an unforgettable story about Helen Grabowski that illustrates the power of the Three C's.

Helen, 81, was mourning the death of her husband of 50-plus years when Joe was referred to her. Her friends and family, worried about her shoveling snow and navigating the stairs in her house, were pressing her to move to a condo. But Joe could tell that selling the house now would be emotionally wrenching for her.

He gave her the same advice he would have given his grandmother. "Mrs. Grabowski, I think you should wait at least a year from your husband's passing before you make a major decision like this," Joe told her. "And a year from now, if you decide to move, I will be happy to sell your home and help you find a condo."

In the meantime, Joe added Helen to his database, contacting her every month with an Item of Value (discussed in the next chapter) and a phone call. He also sent her handwritten notes and did an occasional Pop-By. She even attended one of his Fourth of July client parties. Joe made her the recipient of contact, care, and community.

> *Business trust is built on both character and competence.*

The call from Helen to list her home and find a condo took a little longer than Joe expected—five years, to be precise. It was emotionally challenging for her to sell her home even then, so Joe called her several times a day because he knew she needed to talk. He also stayed in contact with her after she moved into her new condo.

A few years later, Joe received a call from her son, who had recently acquired his real estate license. He told Joe his mother had passed away and asked him to sell her condo.

"Why me?" Joe asked, "Why wouldn't you sell it yourself?"

Helen's son told Joe that he was the executor of his mother's estate. "And it is specified in her will that you be the agent to handle the sale of the property," he said. "She wouldn't trust anyone else to sell her home."

I share this story to illustrate the impact and power of the contact, care, community system. When you use the Three C's to create value through trust, you win the loyalty of your clients. Having demonstrated your character and competence, they recognize your value *and* trust you.

> *When you use the Three C's to create value through trust, you win the loyalty of your clients.*

Applying this system will build a loyal client following. Each and every year, you'll garner more repeat and referral business from your database. And who knows . . . maybe one day someone will write your name into their will as the agent to sell their home.

ACTION STEP

Memorize the Three C's to Success:

- ■ Contact
- ■ Care
- ■ Community

Sales Is a Contact Sport

BY JOE NIEGO

Without promotion, something terrible happens —nothing.

P.T. Barnum

The best prize life offers is the chance to work hard at work worth doing.

Theodore Roosevelt

CHAPTER NINE

Sales Is a Contact Sport

Larry Underhill ventured into real estate after owning two tire shops—one successful, one not—in Lodi, California. His initial introduction to the real estate business was as an investor. The more transactions he did, the more he liked the real estate process, and he eventually became a full-time agent in 1984. Larry loved working with people and the excitement of putting deals together, but he unwittingly became a slave to the Transactional Approach.

"There were days when I knocked on 100 doors in 100-degree heat," says Larry, broker/owner of Statesman Realty in Lodi. "And I punched so many phone numbers that the end of my index finger became flat. I was closing transactions but my tongue was hanging out. I was working too much and enjoying it too little."

Apart from the burnout he was feeling, Larry was increasingly uncomfortable that his lead-generating methods were irritating people, who resented being disturbed at home by a stranger soliciting business.

Thirteen years after he became an agent, Larry made a drastic change in the way he searched for potential clients. "The relational, proactive approach that I learned about at a Turning Point in Monterey, California, resonated with me immediately," he says. "It felt like me and was the way I wanted to treat people as I generated leads."

Instead of knocking on doors all day, Larry spends three hours doing Pop-Bys at the homes of six to eight of his favorite clients. Instead of cold-calling 100 strangers, he checks in daily with 10 people he knows, always remembering to say, "Oh, by the way . . . I'm never too busy for any of your referrals." And instead of an advertising budget, he spends a fraction of those dollars on Items of Value, which he sends to people in his database every month.

Larry became a master at turning the relationships in his database into his own personal sales force, who enthusiastically recommends him to people wanting to buy or sell a house. "I feel now that there is predictability to my income and I have a business I'm proud of," Larry says. "I've done as many as 96 transactions in a single year, and I've dramatically increased my average sale price and my gross commissions without burning myself out. Now I'm teaching the Working by Referral system to all the agents in my office!"

The Recipe Lady or the Agent?

If you flip through the pages of magazines targeted to our industry, you'll find plenty of marketing gimmicks that claim to keep your name foremost in potential clients' minds.

I used them for a while. One year I mailed out baseball schedules for the Chicago Cubs and the White Sox. The next year I sent out football schedules for the Bears. Other agents regularly send out magnetic calendars, jar openers, and ice scrapers—along with everyone else selling a service. But these items fail to highlight your character and competence, which are the key attributes people look for in an agent.

Mary-Jean P. thought she had found the perfect strategy for maintaining contact with her past clients. For more than a decade, she had sent them recipe cards monthly. And when one of her former clients called to say, "I was thinking of you the other day," Mary-Jean silently praised her marketing strategy for doing its job. But her client's next words cut Mary-Jean to the quick. "We just sold our house and bought another. And I wanted to give you our new address so you could continue sending me those wonderful recipe cards!"

In that moment, Mary-Jean realized her recipe cards hadn't done a thing to generate referrals and repeat business from clients. "People thought of me as the lady who sends recipe cards, not the agent to call for their real estate needs," says Mary-Jean. "All that work of sending out cards for 10 years; I was devastated."

Although Mary-Jean's recipes were appreciated by others, they didn't demonstrate her professionalism. Consequently, the people in Mary-Jean's database remembered her culinary interest, not her skill as an agent.

Making Meaningful Contact
Through Items of Value

Buffini & Company has devoted considerable effort to developing what we call Items of Value to remind people in your database *who* you are, *what* you do, and *why* they can trust you with their real estate needs. Unlike baseball schedules or jar openers, which emphasize the *sender* and the *sale*, these items focus on the *recipients* and their *personal concerns*. The message shifts from *buy* to *I care about you*. At the same time, they remind the client that you have the competence they are looking for in an agent or a lender.

Here are three examples of Items of Value you might consider sending to people in your database:

Safeguard Your Identity

Nearly 30 million Americans have been the victims of identity theft, which the FBI calls the fastest-growing type of crime today. "Safeguard Your Identity" (see Figure 4) gives clients practical ways to protect their financial security and privacy. To get them to open the envelope,

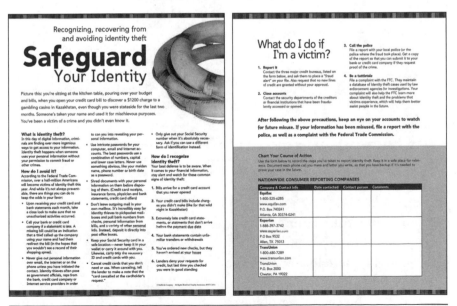

Figure 4. Safeguard Your Identity.

we pose this question in bold print on the front: "Does a thief answer to your name?" The message to clients is that you care for them and are there to help, especially when they face the challenges of buying or selling real estate.

Managing Your Credit Score

Many people are uncertain what their credit score is or how they can improve it. "Managing Your Credit Score" (see Figure 5) gives step-by-step information on how people can enhance their creditworthiness. Improving their credit scores is beneficial for the people in your database as well as for you in working with them on future real estate transactions.

Figure 5. Managing Your Credit Score.

Remodeling Your Home by the Numbers

Every year, the average homeowner spends more than $1,000 on household remodeling projects, and many people spend much more. Total remodeling expenditures exceed $200 billion annually. Not all remodeling, however, contributes to a higher home resale value. Using data from the National Association of the Remodeling Industry, we created "Remodeling Your Home by the Numbers" (see Figure 6) which helps homeowners calculate how much of their remodeling expenses they can recover when they sell.

For other examples and ideas for Items of Value go to www.buffini andcompany.com.

Figure 6. Remodeling Your Home by the Numbers.

Game Plan for Making Systematic Contact

Sending Items of Value will communicate your care and competence, but expressing your desire to receive referrals requires person-to-person contact. You can't just put things in the mail; you've got to call and visit people to truly develop relationships.

Buffini & Company research shows that systematic contact is seven times more effective in generating referrals when it includes regular phone calls. By sending an Item of Value a few days in advance, you've created a natural conversation opener when you phone the recipient. Here's how a call might go:

"Hi Harrison, this is Nolan at Niego Real Estate. I was just check-ing to see if you received the information I sent about identify theft. I don't know if you're aware of it, but identity theft is on the rise and I wouldn't want any of my clients to become victims."

Harrison most likely will express his thanks and if he wants to engage in small talk or exchange updates about family, I will gladly do so. But if not, I keep the call short so I don't waste his time. The primary purpose of the call is to say hello, affirm the value of your relationship, and leave the gentlest of reminders at the end of the call: *"Oh, by the way, Harrison, I'm never too busy for any of your referrals."*

We recommend that you maintain regular contact with the people in your database by sending an Item of Value each month, followed by a phone call. And if you're reluctant to make the calls, remember that there is a big difference between telemarketing firms and you. Telemarketers are trying to sell something. You're merely trying to find people who will be your advocates in recommending your great service to those who need it.

Turning Contacts into Referrals

Maintaining regular contact also provides you with an opportunity to build your business by:

- Educating clients on how the real estate industry works
- Articulating how you work
- Outlining the specific benefits that your clients enjoy

Brian and I have created the following Referral Dialog to help you communicate these points. This Dialog is best used when first meet-ing a client to explain how you work and to differentiate yourself from others in the marketplace.

Educate your clients on how the industry works
"You know, most people in the real estate business spend the majori-ty of their time and resources prospecting for new business by doing things like cold-calling, door-knocking, sending direct mail, and buy-ing advertising."

Articulate how you work

"I want to devote myself to serving the needs of my clients before, during, and after each transaction. I would like to ask that you refer people to me who would be great to work with. If you know anyone who is thinking of buying or selling a home and would appreciate the same level of attention I have given you, please give me their name and business number and I'll be happy to follow up and take great care of them."

Outline the benefits to the client

"You see, as long as you and my other clients keep referring me, I can continue working with good people like you. And instead of knocking on doors, I can do an even better job of serving you."

You can adjust this Dialog to suit your own speaking style and the client's situation. The purpose of this Dialog is to help clients see why referrals make sense for you and for *them*.

Making a Lasting Impression

While Brian was growing up in Dublin painting houses with his father, my four brothers and I spent our summer breaks from high school working in our family's one-truck concrete business. My father, Ron Niego, owned Meta Concrete, which poured hundreds of miles of sidewalks and driveways throughout Chicago's South Side.

My dad taught me that the quality of the preparation work we did before we poured the concrete would determine how long the work would last. Although enduring quality wouldn't be apparent to customers initially, my dad insisted that we go the extra mile to give our customers true value and to never cut corners.

While we were putting the final touches on a newly poured sidewalk or driveway, my dad would assess our work and only when it met his standard did he impress "Meta Concrete" and our home phone number into the fresh concrete with a brass stamp. Today, when I go to the South Side of Chicago, I can still see some of the thousands of impressions we made by literally putting our name on our work.

My father didn't spend money on advertising. He did good work and let his reputation speak for itself. In time, past clients referred him to new clients, who referred him to others. To this day, when people on Chicago's South Side think of concrete, our family's company often comes to mind.

I want you to experience the same customer loyalty in your business. When you have done great work for a client, you need to keep that memory vivid in your client's mind. Just like my father's brass stamp, the monthly Items of Value and follow-up calls will create a lasting positive impression. Instead of thinking of you as the "recipe person" or never thinking of you at all, your competence as an agent or lender will always come to mind.

ACTION STEPS

- Establish which Items of Value you will use to make contact with your database each month. Make sure it communicates your character and competence.

- To learn more about our Referral System's Lead-Generation Kit and get ready-to-mail Items of Value, visit www.buffiniandcompany.com.

- Memorize The Referral Dialog and use it during the follow-up call.

Care: Moving Beyond Buying and Selling

By Brian Buffini

*Treat other people exactly as you would like
to be treated by them…*

Matthew 7:12

No act of kindness, no matter how small is ever wasted.

Aesop

CHAPTER TEN

Care: Moving Beyond Buying and Selling

Like most Americans on September 11, 2001, Paul Hunter stared transfixed at his television screen as images played over and over of the World Trade Center in New York being attacked by suicide bombers and later collapsing. Only a few miles from his home in northern Virginia, the Pentagon was in flames from another terrorist attack.

Beyond his outrage and shock over the attack that shook Americans' security to the core, Paul also struggled with another deep foreboding. Only 10 days earlier he'd received his real estate license. Starting a new real estate career in the aftermath of 9/11 was definitely bad timing.

Although Paul had been earning a substantial salary as an IT executive, frequent travel took him away from his wife and two young children, and he feared that he would miss too much of his family's life. When Hunter and his wife, Andrea, mulled over the types of careers that offered flexible hours, unlimited income potential, and the ability to be his own boss, selling real estate topped the list.

Now Paul obsessed over the jeopardy in which he had placed his family's financial future as he watched the airline industry ground all commercial flights, the stock market tank, and anthrax infiltrate the postal system. Maybe his former colleagues were right when they told him he was crazy for abandoning his swift climb up the corporate ladder. How could he have been so irresponsible to switch to real estate when there were no prospective clients in sight?

Andrea, watching her husband consumed by stress, told him she would be willing to sell their new house and live in an apartment so he could stop worrying about the mortgage and focus all his energy on getting his new career off the ground. His wife's belief in him and offer to sacrifice the family's comfort fueled Paul's motivation—he vowed to succeed, no matter what the circumstances.

A fellow agent referred Paul to a Turning Point in Tyson's Corner, Virginia, where he learned about the Working by Referral system. Paul jettisoned the passive-cold and proactive-cold sales approaches he'd been using and started building and qualifying his database. He learned Dialogs to help him better communicate his requests for referrals. And he wrote a personal note to each of the 128 people in his database.

During the holiday season, he did a number of Pop-Bys. People in a community still reeling from their close encounter with terrorism opened, read, and appreciated Paul's handwritten notes and were impressed with the time he took to visit them.

As a result of Paul's heartfelt care and concern for the people in his database, he began receiving a steady stream of referrals. Paul closed over $13 million in production his first full year in the business. And the Hunter family has never again given thought to selling their home.

Giving Against the Grain

One of the biggest complaints people have about agents is their apparent lack of concern for their clients. "All they care about is closing the deal and cashing the commission check," is an all too-frequent gripe.

In part, that lack of care is due to what Thomas L. Friedman, author of the bestselling "The World Is Flat" and a columnist for *The New York Times*, calls "continuous partial attention." We're all moving so quickly and monitoring multiple tasks simultaneously that we fail to give our full attention to anything.

Agents are some of the biggest practitioners of continuous partial attention. As you drive to a closing, what are you thinking about? Probably not how you are going to maintain an ongoing relationship with your clients, who, by the way, may think you are the best thing since sliced bread. You're probably thinking about the next deal and where you're going to find it. Without any future expression of care from you, your clients may feel deserted and forgotten. Your opportunity to receive referrals from that couple just vanished.

You can, however, replace continuous partial attention to your clients with consistent intentional attention by staying in touch with them, writing notes to everyone in your database, and doing Pop-Bys.

The Power of the Written Word

The most powerful and least expensive way to deepen a relationship with a client is to send a handwritten personal note—a rare find in anyone's mailbox these days.

Personal notes have been the cornerstone of our business for 20 years but now, more than ever, they represent true value to our clients. Surrounded by so much slick direct-mail advertising, computerized phone messages, and mass e-mail messages, people crave the human connection and intimacy that a handwritten note conveys.

A handwritten note will always get read. I can't imagine tossing one in the trash can without opening it. And neither will your clients. Yes, note writing does take time. But if you're consistent about carving out a small amount of time every day to write them, the task won't consume you. Keep a stack of note cards and envelopes on your desk, and each morning before you check your e-mail messages, write a pre-determined number of notes. Three notes a day add up to 15 a week or 60 a month. Imagine making 60 meaningful impressions on your client base every month!

Surrounded by so much slick direct-mail advertising, computerized phone messages, and mass e-mail messages, people crave the human connection and intimacy that a handwritten note conveys.

The message from a handwritten note lingers, unlike an e-mail message that is often quickly deleted. A good note isn't about expressing yourself, however. It's about listening to your clients and writing something that will resonate with their needs, hurts, or desires.

Make the note personal. Mention the kids by name or the family dog who kept nudging your arm asking for another pat on the head. Thank them for the referral they sent you, taking the time to meet, or the coffee and donuts you shared. And make sure you write the note in your own handwriting, even if it's less than perfect.

> *If you're a new agent and don't yet have any clients, you can certainly write a two- or three-sentence note to people in your database "just to stay in touch."*

After an appointment, it's a good idea to jot down a few thoughts so that you don't forget the personal details about someone to whom you'll send a note. Also, send a personal note after your Item of Value follow-up call to the people in your database. Remember to stay on top of your notes and don't let the demands of the day deter you from writing a few every day.

If you're a new agent and don't yet have any clients, you can certainly write a two- or three-sentence note to people in your database "just to stay in touch." Go to www.buffiniandcompany.com for examples of personal notes that Joe and I have written. Paul Hunter would undoubtedly vouch for the power of a handwritten personal note—and the need to write them every day.

Let me share with you a favorite story that shows the power of a personal note. I received a call from Bill, a past client. He wanted to refer me to his father's friend. After relaying as much information as he had, Bill added, "Be as gentle as you can Brian; this man just lost his wife."

After thanking him, I put a call in to William M. and after a short conversation, he invited me to view his home. As I met Will at the door, I asked him to give me a tour of his home. As we walked from room to room, it was apparent he was more interested in showing me pictures of his kids and grandkids that hung on every wall. Every third or fourth sentence, he would mention his late wife, Miriam.

Eventually we wound up at the kitchen table. As we began to discuss the prospect of listing his house for sale, he became quite emotional. I called my assistant to re-schedule an appointment that was making me feel rushed, sat back down and said, "Let's forget about your house right now. Tell me all about your family."

He relaxed, and began to tell me about his wife of 46 years and how she had waited for him while he served in World War II. He talked about their kids and their first home—all the stories interspersed with memories of Kennedy's assassin, the Vietnam War and the 1980 U.S. Hockey Team–Miracle on Ice.

Will had seen a lot of life and I thoroughly enjoyed our time together, but a thought kept haunting me: Will didn't seem interested in moving to be with his daughter. He seemed more resigned to moving on to be with his wife.

Upon leaving, I told him I would be in touch to further discuss the sale of his home when he was ready. When I got back to my office, I wrote Will a thank you note. I thanked him for showing me his home, and also let him know how he had inspired me. I told him I hoped that after 46 years of marriage, I would still be in love with my wife the way he was with his.

Three months later we listed and sold his house and he moved to Ohio to be with his daughter.

Fifteen years later, I got a phone call over the Christmas Holidays from Will's daughter to let me know her father had passed. She wanted me to know that when they read his eulogy from his personal Bible, the bookmark he used for his daily scripture readings was the letter I had sent all those years ago. "We read the letter," she said, "It must have made quite an impact on him."

Never underestimate the power of the personal note. Sometimes it's just what someone needs to hear that day.

Making Contact Face to Face

Staying in contact with people is a key to Working by Referral. Sending a personal note has a big impact and is a highly leveraged activity. And when done in conjunction with Pop-Bys, you deepen the relationships in your database overnight.

A Pop-By is a method we use to stay connected on a person-to-person basis. Unlike a personal note, a Pop-By is interactive. You get a chance to look into a person's eyes, shake their hand, and ask them how they are doing. And since 75 percent of all communication is nonverbal, you can convey much more in a Pop-By than you can in a personal note. By your mere presence, a Pop-By communicates that you value the relationship and care enough to invest your time on a visit.

> *By your mere presence, a Pop-By communicates that you value the relationship and care enough to invest your time on a visit.*

Doing a Pop-By is easy: You visit your favorite people in your database and bring them a simple token of appreciation. Since Pop-Bys take more time and energy than making a call or writing a note, reserve them for your A+ and A clients.

Politely give the person you will visit advance notice such as, "I'm going to be in your area tomorrow and I'd love to Pop-By between 2 and 3 p.m. I'll just stop for a minute."

When you arrive, leave your car in the driveway with the engine running while you briefly chat at the front door and present them with a token of appreciation. As you depart, say, "Oh, by the way®. . . " and remind them that you're never too busy for any referrals.

You can adapt Pop-Bys to the season or holiday. For example, the week before Mother's Day, drop by with a small bouquet of flowers or a potted plant. This is a fun and personally rewarding exercise. Imagine delivering flowers to 150 mothers, getting hugged all day, and generating business at the same time.

> *Pop-Bys are an opportunity for you to tap into your personal creativity and flair.*

Pop-Bys are an opportunity for you to tap into your personal creativity and flair. If you're a great cook, deliver one of your special dishes. Maybe you're a master gardener, have a deep interest in music, or once worked in a different profession where you had a particular expertise. Leverage your uniqueness and create tokens of appreciation that best reflect your character and your competence. Give of who you are, not of what you have. For more ideas on Pop-By gifts go to www.buffiniandcompany.com.

A Message from "The Pop-By Queen"

Mary Beth Eisenhard of Gainesville, Virginia, is often thought of as the "Pop-By Queen."

After retiring as Lieutenant Colonel in the U.S. Army, Mary Beth and her husband, Scot, left Fort Reilly, Kansas and bought a home in Thousand Oaks, California in 1993. Searching for a new career, Mary Beth accepted her real estate agent's offer to be her assistant. In 1994, she got her real estate license and ventured off on her own.

"My first few months on my own, I had doubts whether I had what it takes to be successful in this business," recalls Mary Beth. "I knew I loved socializing with people, but I didn't know how to use my social skills to generate leads." Then Mary Beth attended the Turning Point and discovered Pop-Bys, which she credits with launching her real estate career. "Making phone calls and writing notes are activities I struggle to do consistently. I would much rather visit with people," she says.

Some of her favorite Pop-By gifts have been holiday music CDs, heart-shaped cookies on Valentine's Day, and home-made pumpkin bread in the fall.

Just as Mary Beth began gaining confidence that she was going to be successful as a real estate agent, Scot's job transferred to Huntsville, Alabama. Not knowing a soul in Huntsville, Mary Beth once again had to build her real estate business from the bottom up with two tools: her ease with people and the tried-and-true Pop-Bys.

Just as business started to take off in Huntsville, her husband transferred once again, this time to northern Virginia. Starting up a new real estate business for the third time, Mary Beth again relied on Pop-Bys to build referrals. "Even though the housing market is different in the three states I've worked, Pop-Bys have allowed me to use my personality to build a successful real estate business wherever I go," says Mary Beth.

"This year I will close over $8 million in production," she says. "Hopefully we won't get transferred again. But if we do, even at age 54 I have no fear of starting over because I have Pop-Bys in my arsenal!"

Keep That Referral Point of View

I can hear some of you now saying, "Hey, my main business is selling homes. But now these guys want me to become my city's social director!" We understand your concern. But as we've said before, you are not in the house business, you're in the business of generating leads. And if you want to succeed, you need to devote a significant chunk of your time and energy caring for the people who will refer leads to you.

You don't need to take a course on interpersonal communication to make a phone call, write a note, or do a Pop-By. But if calling on people makes you anxious at first, role-play with a family member or friend. All you are really doing is greeting someone with a smile and extending your hand with a token gift. Be personable, say hello, ask how they are doing, and talk about the small gift you brought. Remember to end with, "Oh, by the way . . . I'm never too busy to take care of your referrals."

If Paul Hunter could be successful generating referrals immediately after 9/11, when many people in Virginia didn't want to open their mail or their doors because of terrorism and anthrax, you surely can, too.

ACTION STEP

Pop-By 15 of your favorite clients. Check out
www.buffiniandcompany.com for Pop-By gift ideas.
Afterward, send each one of your clients a hand-written,
personal note.

CHAPTER ELEVEN

Community:
Creating a
Client for Life

BY BRIAN BUFFINI

Every business is built on friendship.
J. C. Penny

Our favorite holding period is forever.
Warren Buffett

Community: Creating a Client for Life

I like Merriam-Webster's definition of community as a body of persons of common interests scattered through a larger society. People want to connect with like-minded individuals and socialize with those who have similar interests. In this chapter, we will delve into the social aspects of community. In Chapter 12 we will explore the business-networking opportunity inside community.

Worries over her husband's cardiac condition and her own financial future led Phyllis Glover to abandon a 20-year career teaching high school and college English to pursue a real estate license. "If my husband was unable to work, I didn't know how I would pay the mortgage on a teacher's salary," says Phyllis of Dallas, Texas. "Plus, I needed a more flexible work schedule than teaching allowed."

When Phyllis started selling real estate in 1985, interest rates hovered at 15 percent, foreclosures were hitting record highs, and agents were exiting the profession. "I felt like I was all dressed up to go to the party, but nobody was there," recalls Phyllis.

Where was she going to find clients in such a dismal real estate market? Phyllis turned to geographical farming to develop leads. "There were over 2,000 people in my geographical farm," she says. "It was costly and I wasn't building relationships."

Then Phyllis' Buffini & Company Business Coach, Carol Peterson, challenged her to focus on community, one of the Three C's. The idea was to strategically build a sense of community among the people in Phyllis' database as a way of generating referrals. Phyllis chose to throw client parties to create a deeper fellowship among her contacts. Although she had held sporadic client parties in the past, she became very adept at hosting them once they became integrated into her business practices.

Over the years, Phyllis and her husband, Curtis, have used their love of travel to lend an exotic atmosphere to the parties. "When we visited Alaska, we purchased party favors for a party with an Alaskan theme," she says. "We did the same in Greece, China, Italy, India, and Russia, to name a few."

The couple encourages guests to dress in costumes based on the party's country theme, they serve traditional food and drink from that country, and they decorate the room to make attendees feel as if they are in a foreign place. "My clients love the parties; they even encourage me to go on vacation so I can throw another themed party with what I bring back from my travels," says Phyllis.

But the parties are more than simply fun for Phyllis, who closed over $20 million in production in 2007. "Client parties generate goodwill within my business," she says. "Last year, 92 percent of my business came from referrals. I will do client parties for the rest of my career."

The Power of Community

In 2000, public policy expert Robert D. Putnam published one of the most discussed books of recent times, *Bowling Alone: The Collapse and Revival of American Community*. Putnam examines the trend of Americans becoming more solitary, evidenced by declining memberships in clubs, unions, churches, and volunteer activities. Over the past quarter century, the number of people attending club meetings has dropped 58 percent, entertaining friends at home has diminished by 45 percent, and a third fewer families report sharing regular family dinners.

Business transactions have also radically changed. Most business deals 25 years ago were made face to face, providing plenty of opportunities for personal contact and free exchange of ideas. But today our interactions are more virtual than social as e-mail and the Internet have replaced meetings and phone calls.

Yet although so many of us may be "bowling alone," we still crave community. Witness the tremendous growth of social networking sites like Facebook and MySpace, which have attracted millions of users. This clearly demonstrates individuals' built-in desire to connect, but it also serves as a reminder that the age-old places of connection are not satisfying the needs of people any longer. Today people have a hard time meeting one another, which has resulted in the incredible growth of dating Web sites, for example.

By hosting social events, you can create a vibrant community network with the people in your database, strengthening relationships and building loyalty.

Agents and lenders are in an excellent position to restore some of that connectedness that is so lacking today. By hosting social events, you can create a vibrant community network with the people in your database, strengthening relationships and building loyalty. Your clients' lives will be richer for it and so will your business. In fact, fostering community is essential to your business.

Building Community Through Client Parties

Like any personal relationship, the greater the contact with the people in your database, the stronger their bond will be with you. Think about the concept of breaking bread and how significant it is to building relationships. The major holidays like Thanksgiving, Hanukkah, Christmas, and Easter are always centered on a great meal. People developing a romantic relationship frequently share a meal. And besides, any system developed by Irishmen must have an emphasis on eating and drinking!

Client parties allow you to give generously to those in your database and make it more comfortable to ask for referrals later. Your parties will also provide a chance for folks to interact with like-minded people, so they'll have a great experience, too.

We realize that some of the suggestions below for client parties can be pricey. But with a little creativity, you can keep the cost to a minimum and still show people a good time. Here are a few examples of client parties that have worked well for us.

Housewarming party

While you're working with buyers, mention that you'd like to host a housewarming party for them two to four months after they move into their new home. Once they close the deal, offer to send out the invitations, call all the guests, and provide finger food, refreshments, and desserts. (Skip the alcohol.)

When your clients' friends come to the party and share in the excitement of a new home, some may be inspired to think about finding a new house of their own.

When your clients' friends come to the party and share in the excitement of a new home, some may be inspired to think about finding a new house of their own. They are also getting a first-hand look at how you treat your clients and probably wondering why their agents never gave them housewarming parties after they bought their homes.

After the party, call the attendees to thank them for joining the celebration and to ask the Mayor Campaign question: "If you were buying or selling a home, or had a family member or friend who was, do you have an agent you'd refer them to?" Chances are several will say No, so you've just realized an opportunity to increase the size of your database.

Client appreciation party

I use this party to deepen the connection with my past clients and my A clients as well as other relationships I've developed through my business. This is typically an annual event designed to thank them for their support, continuing patronage, and for their referrals. It gives you a chance to go all out if you'd like.

We've seen agents host casino-theme nights, costume parties, summer events, ethnic fests, and tailgate parties. I opt for a Fourth of July party, which dovetails with our company's practice of distributing 16,000 American flags throughout the neighborhood. The party is a lot of fun and generates referrals for us each year. If you would like to see pictures from my Client Appreciation Party go to www.buffiniandcompany.com.

It's important to note that parties greatly add to the compounding effect on your business. In addition to the calls, notes, Pop-Bys, and Items of Value, parties serve as a catalyst for referred business.

Business mixer

Every business owner welcomes the opportunity to increase customer referrals through networking. Plan a mixer with punch and finger food and invite all the business owners in your database as well as owners of companies to whom you refer clients.

Tell them you'd like to introduce local business owners—including yourself—so they can get to know one another and perhaps refer customers. (Some of your guests may be willing to share the costs of a networking party.)

A⁺ client party

This party is a more intimate and possibly lavish gathering for those who consistently send you referrals. Your business owes them a debt of gratitude, so generously reward them. Rent a private room in an exclusive restaurant, invite them to your home and hire a chef, or perhaps rent a yacht for an evening's dinner cruise. It's important that, in addition to all the other parties and perks your business provides, you take time to set aside a unique experience for this special group of people.

Vendor celebrations

Why not invite your vendors to a party? On average, there are 26 services involved 30 days before, during and 30 days after a real estate transaction: contractors to decorators, accountants to movers, and everything in between.

These people typically serve not just you, but many other professionals in the real estate space. Yet their work often goes without thanks or appreciation. When you throw a party for this group, it distinguishes you from the other agents with whom they work. Also, the vast majority of agents aren't going to be asking for their referrals, which sets you apart and puts you in a good position to make clients of vendors and their friends. And building a sense of connection with these service providers creates a team environment as you work together throughout the year.

Building Community Through Business Lunches

> *The one-on-one interaction can cement a relationship and business lunches are easy to fit into the workday.*

Taking someone to lunch creates an opportunity to build community in your database, one relationship at a time. The one-on-one interaction can cement a relationship and business lunches are easy to fit into the workday.

We've found that people who run smaller businesses and service industries are often starving for information on generating their own leads and referrals. Here is the Dialog our Coaches recommend when inviting a business owner to lunch:

"Hi Anthony, this is Anna of Jackson Realty. I don't know if I mentioned it to you, but I'm currently using a Business Coach to help me devise ways to increase my referrals. I was thinking that this information might be very helpful in your business and I'd be happy to share it with you. Does this sound like something you'd be interested in? Why don't we get together for lunch, and I'll bring my Coaching manual to show you what I'm learning."

If you are having lunch with vendors, be sure to let them know that you refer people to them when you can, and then ask them for their referrals. The law of reciprocity benefits you and the vendor.

Some of you may already be taking business associates to lunch on a regular basis, but perhaps you could do so in a more strategic manner in order to build a stronger business-to-business community network. This benefits not just you, but also the others you incorporate into the community.

Partying His Way to the Top

Upon graduating from Baylor University with a degree in business administration, Morgan Davis was quickly recruited by EDS, a company founded by Ross Perot, in Plano, Texas.

Morgan spent two years working as a systems analyst before deciding he wanted a career that was more relational. He thought he had found it when he joined the staff of Young Life, a Christian youth outreach ministry program for the inner city kids of Portland, Oregon. But the financial demands of a growing family eventually forced Morgan to look for another opportunity. A friend in the real estate business, who had a Buffini & Company Coach, recognized Morgan's talents and hired him as an assistant.

"I was exploding with excitement and passion for the potential this business offered," says Morgan, who soon became an agent. "I learned about the power of the Working by Referral system and was anxious to harness it."

Morgan implemented every aspect of the Working by Referral system. He built his database, then sorted and qualified it. He faithfully does the calls, notes and Pop-Bys. He memorized the Dialogs and uses them every time he interacts with a client. And he throws grand client parties that no one wants to miss.

Every October, with the help of his staff and a few friends, he hosts a party with catered food, game show-like entertainment, and recognition and awards for his top referral sources. Last year, every one of his 200 guests left with a fleece jacket as a gift. The only way to attend this gala event is to have bought or sold a home with Morgan, or sent him a referral.

"The volume of referrals I receive peaks every year during the months of August, September, and October," Morgan, 45, explains. "I guess everyone wants to guarantee an invitation to the party."

Although referrals have resulted in production of over $40 million a year for Morgan, he doesn't intend for his party to be simply a referral generator. "My client party is an excellent opportunity for me to spend time with my clients and a gracious way to say thank you for trusting me with their real estate business," he says. "This business can often make you feel like you're all alone. The wonderful thing about Working by Referral is building a feeling of community with people in your database who are willing to refer you, endorse you, and be your advocates. I'm not chasing clients; I'm surrounded by friends."

ACTION STEP

Choose of one of the Community Strategies and execute on it.
(Circle one)

- Housewarming Party
- Client Appreciation Party
- Business Mixer
- A⁺ Client Party
- Vendor Celebration
- Business Lunch

CHAPTER TWELVE

Taking Care
of Business

BY BRIAN BUFFINI

Alone we can do so little; together we can do so much.
Helen Keller

In business for yourself, not by yourself.
Ray Kroc

Taking Care of Business

As Neville G. sat in the reception area of one of the largest banks in Southern California, he stared down at his scrubbed hands, which still held stubborn traces of black tar from his roofing business. He had on a suit for the first time since marrying his bride 11 years before. But despite his pending appointment with Frank S., the bank's president, he wasn't at all nervous. Frank and Neville already had a great relationship. When the bank repossessed a foreclosed property, Neville knew he'd get a call to inspect the roof and remedy any problems.

I was also at this appointment at the encouragement of Neville, whose roofing business I had been promoting to people in my database for several years. Neville's business was also included in my referral directory of the best San Diego businesses. As we were ushered into the president's office, I couldn't help but notice a two-foot stack of brochures and promotional pieces from real estate agents in the corner of Frank's office. I was also courting the bank's business, but I was taking a very different tack. Neville made the introductions and proceeded to describe my business and how I served my clients and facilitated referrals to numerous businesses in town. Within 15 minutes, I had acquired my biggest client.

"We take Neville's endorsement very seriously, Brian, since we know him so well," said Frank. "We're averaging 10 foreclosures a month right now and are in need of a good agent to represent us. Let's get started on a couple of listings to see how we all work together."

Over the next four years, I sold dozens of homes for this bank—often to buyers from my database that I had been cultivating.

What a lucky break for Brian, you may be thinking. But luck had little to do with it. I had paved the way for my relationship with the bank by actively driving leads to Neville's roofing business, and when he had an opportunity to reciprocate, he was more than happy to do so.

And I was extremely grateful to have the bank as a client during the challenging San Diego real estate market in the early '90s. With the Cold War over, many local defense contractors instituted massive layoffs, which caused many people to leave the city. Interest rates also skyrocketed and housing prices plummeted 30 percent. But although more than half the agents on my local real estate board left the business under these difficult conditions, my net income tripled between 1990 and 1995. The reason for my success: 40 percent of my income came from referrals from the solid business-to-business network I had built.

I found that it was relatively easy to ask business owners for referrals—especially if I was already referring my customers to them. My business contacts also brought me a higher-quality clientele, which increased my average sales price. These referred people were highly motivated to use me for their real estate needs because the endorsement I had received was both a personal and professional one.

Networking with Business Owners

You undoubtedly have your own business network in place; the average real estate transaction, as we've said, involves 26 services. (Go to www.buffiniandcompany.com for the complete list of services.) But to capitalize on those relationships, you need to nurture them so your business associates have an incentive to refer their customers to you. Here are some ways to ensure that your business associates are always thinking of you when someone they know needs an agent or lender.

Join more groups
Perhaps you're already part of a networking organization in your local area. But now that you realize the power of business referrals, you may want to investigate becoming an active member of additional groups, such as BNI, Kiwanis, and your chamber of commerce.

Host a business mixer

Business people enjoy being with each other. By hosting a mixer of local business owners, you make yourself the central hub in a community of closely connected people. After all, the two things everyone in the room will have in common are owning a business and their relationship with you.

Seek out social gatherings

One of the major mistakes I see agents make is taking themselves out of circulation. Early in their careers they probably enthusiastically networked at social functions. But as their client rosters grew, they preferred the comfort of sitting in their offices instead of making the effort to meet new people. But guess what? The people with whom you share an office aren't going to use you to buy or sell their homes. So overcome your inertia and accept those invitations to socialize.

> *One of the major mistakes I see agents make is taking themselves out of circulation.*

Learn together

Real estate professionals are inundated with offers to attend personal and professional development courses, probably more so than other business people. Invite three or four business owners in your community to attend a seminar that is of interest to all of you. Spending the day together is a great opportunity to deepen your relationship so that asking for referrals comes naturally.

Put on a seminar

I would often host a seminar for people in my database on a topic such as how to buy investment real estate. I'd ask my financial planner and accountant to be guest speakers and prepared marketing materials to entice people to attend.

During the event, the accountant outlined the tax benefits and strategies of investing, the financial planner discussed owning real estate as part of an overall investment portfolio, and I would show specific examples of homes on the market with investment potential. The accountant, financial planner, and I all benefited from referrals as a result of the seminar.

Break bread together

Everyone, no matter how busy, has to eat. Consider that every significant social event in life is accompanied by food, so it's no wonder that people who share a meal together usually forge a more intimate connection with each other. Make sure your calendar is filled up with breakfasts, lunches, or coffees dates with business owners you can refer your customers to and who will reciprocate in kind.

Build a business directory

The cornerstone of my business-to-business strategy was the directory I created listing all the best tradespeople and services in San Diego, which became a resource for every homeowner.

The businesses in the directory were compiled by recommendations from those in my database as well as from my personal experiences. I sent everyone in my database a letter titled "Help me help you" asking them for all the local businesses they endorsed. (Go to www.buffiniandcompany.com to see a copy of the letter.) Over 78 people in my database responded by phone to tell my assistant about an experience they had with a particular business.

My directory grew with all the names of businesses the people in my database endorsed as superior, making it a valuable resource for everyone who received it. But the names also expanded my network of businesses I could refer my customers to—and potentially get referrals from them.

Assembling the directory also allowed me to discover the super-advocates in my database. When someone convincingly sells you on the merits of a particular restaurant, you get a pretty good idea how they might extol your attributes as an agent. This went from being my business directory to being our business directory as it became a must-have for my community of clients.

If you're just starting to build your business network, I recommend compiling a Top 10 list of the businesses you refer customers to and send it to the people in your database as an Item of Value. As the list grows, you can print it as a directory or post it on your Web site.

ACTION STEPS

Collect a list of the Top Ten Businesses you refer or have the potential to refer. These businesses will be the foundation of your Business Directory.

1. _____
2. _____
3. _____
4. _____
5. _____
6. _____
7. _____
8. _____
9. _____
10. _____

Add these names to your database.
Go to www.buffiniandcompany.com to learn about generating more referrals from your business directory.

Section III

Taking Action

Winning the Day

BY JOE NIEGO

There is no one giant step that does it.
It's a lot of little steps.

Peter A. Cohen

You don't just luck into things as much as you would like
to think you do. You build step by step, whether it is
friendships or opportunities.

Barbara Bush

Winning the Day

To watch the movie "The March of the Penguins" is to be awestruck at the dogged determination displayed by the emperor penguins of Antarctica during their annual breeding migration. At the onset of the mating season, the male and female penguins will travel some 70 miles over rough terrain to their breeding grounds. After mating, the female transfers her egg to her mate for safekeeping and waddles and slides another 70 miles to feed in open water for the first time in two months. Meanwhile, the males huddle together on the ice, braving temperatures of minus 80 degrees and winds of 200 mph, to guard the eggs. By the time the males make their own 70-mile trek to eat after the females return, they've lost half their body weight.

Summing up this ritual of selfless devotion, the film's narrator, Morgan Freeman, says, "In the harshest place on earth, love finds a way." The penguins achieve this herculean goal by using the strategy that I use in my real estate business called "winning the day."

How do these birds accomplish such a seemingly daunting task? By taking one step at a time, one day at a time. Just like these "land-challenged" animals, you need to focus on making measurable progress in generating leads each day in order to accomplish your production goals.

> *You need to focus on making measurable progress in generating leads each day in order to accomplish your production goals*

In this chapter, I will share the five habits you must incorporate into your business to keep you motivated and focused on winning the day. But first you must agree to abandon the "microwave mentality."

No Shortcuts to Generating Leads

When Amana introduced the $495 home microwave oven more than 40 years ago, the Radarange not only revolutionized the way people cooked, it forever changed how we view time. Wanting everything instantly—meals, the perfect physique, career and financial success—is a result of what I and others term the "microwave mentality."

Our TV dramas solve complex problems in 30 or 60 minutes, and advertisers would have us believe that improving self-esteem can be achieved immediately with the right car or toothpaste. So it's no surprise that people who attend our Turning Points arrive with a microwave mentality, hoping we'll reveal the secret to instant success.

I'm sorry to say that a formula for an instant career transformation doesn't exist. Anything touted as a "quick fix" will likely result in dashed expectations when success doesn't materialize. And the sense of failure these schemes engender gives rise to negative momentum. This can cause us to lose the day, the week, the month, and ultimately the year.

> *The only way to make lasting change is to foster winning habits. And the single most important habit for a real estate professional to develop is to execute lead-generation activities every single workday.*

The only way to make lasting change is to foster winning habits. And the single most important habit for a real estate professional to develop is to execute lead-generation activities every single workday:

- Making check-in calls with clients and people in your database
- Writing personal notes
- Doing Pop-Bys
- Adding new people to your database

Naturally there will be days when you simply can't find the time or energy to generate leads. Our advice, however, is to make this the exception to the rule.

120

Vince Lombardi, the famed coach of the Green Bay Packers, knew something about the rewards of practicing good habits. "Winning is not a sometime thing; it's an all time thing," he said. "You don't win once in a while, you don't do things right once in a while, you do them right all the time. Winning is habit. Unfortunately, so is losing."

Following are the habits you need to develop in order to win the day.

Habit 1: Focus on your goals

Have you ever experienced emotional swings during a week in real estate? If you are like me, you may have a few clients who buy and a couple listings that sell. That puts you on top of the world! Then, you get a client with buyer's remorse who wants out of a deal—after you've been working with him for three months. Next, the home inspector says the sold listing you've had on the market for six months has mold in the attic and a bad heat exchanger in the furnace; the buyers want their earnest money returned. You schedule an appointment with the dentist just to alleviate your stress.

In our business, you have to accept a certain amount of turbulence. But if you neglect making calls, writing notes, and doing Pop-Bys during the rough patches, you'll lose first one day, followed by another, and pretty soon you've lost several weeks. Now you have no listings or buyers to work with, all because you took your eye off the prize.

> *In our business, you have to accept a certain amount of turbulence.*

When I am feeling tired and a little down, I use my goals to inspire me to win the day. I always carry my annual goals with me on a 3 x 5 card and refer to them whenever I need a boost. Here are a few of my goals:

- Fully fund educational savings accounts for my children
- Contribute the maximum amount to my retirement account
- Purchase one piece of investment real estate each year
- Hire help for Julie (my wife) with the kids
- Go on a "date night" with Julie every week

- Donate to causes I believe in
- Close 225 transactions this year

So if I don't win the day, I know that I'm shortchanging my children's education, the amount of time I spend with Julie, my retirement nest egg, and my charitable intentions.

> *Many agents aim for nothing and hit it with amazing accuracy. Setting clear goals is crucial to wanting to succeed.*

Why do the penguins march 70 miles? For them, it's a matter of survival. Why do you sell real estate? Many agents aim for nothing and hit it with amazing accuracy. Setting clear goals is crucial to wanting to succeed.

At our seminars, Brian and I have helped over a million people set meaningful goals, and we receive hundreds of notes each year from agents and lenders sharing how their goals kept them focused on winning the day and bring meaning to their work.

Habit 2: Structure your work

Perhaps the most attractive aspect of the real estate business is the personal freedom and flexibility it offers agents and lenders. As independent contractors, we are our own bosses and can work the hours we choose. But that very freedom is part of the reason our industry turns over 70 percent of its sales force every three years. People who define freedom as working without structure aren't going to make it in this field. To be successful, you have to run your business like a business and treat it as a job. And that requires structured work habits.

> *To be successful, you have to run your business like a business and treat it as a job.*

Early in my career I discovered that the more structure I had in my day, the more freedom and flexibility I experienced. That's not as contradictory as it sounds. By blocking off two hours a day for phone calls, notes and Pop-Bys, I received the treasured referrals I was after. I also spent less and earned more.

Brian and I could write an entire book on how to structure your schedule, but let me give you a few ideas to consider.

Start time:

Most agents head into the office whenever the spirit moves them. But establishing a consistent time to start your day is one of the most productive things you can do. For me it is 9:00 a.m. The time doesn't have to be early; it just needs to be scheduled.

Breaks:

It is extremely difficult to be 100-percent productive all day long. I've always scheduled two 30-minute breaks into my day. The perfect time for me is right after an hour of generating leads.

Lunch:

Two-hour lunches are not uncommon among agents. Leisurely lunches are fine now and then, but just make sure you schedule them so they don't become a daily event.

Handling transactions:

The follow-through on a transaction can consume your entire day if you let it. Be proactive and schedule time to make all calls regarding transactions uninterrupted. Leave a detailed message for the person you're calling, and ask for a detailed message in return.

Day's end:

You probably head home from the office every day feeling guilty because there is at least one task left undone. That feeling will never go away; I still have it after 20 years. Learning to manage the guilt has been key for me, however. If I'm not listing a property, writing a contract, or presenting a contract, any tasks that are pending can wait until tomorrow. You must schedule the time your day will end for your sake as well as your family's.

Time blocking:

The most important habit to develop to ensure that you spend two hours a day generating leads is time blocking. This is a technique of scheduling uninterrupted time to execute an activity, which, in this case, involves making calls, writing notes, and doing Pop-Bys. You can be flexible about when you schedule your time block, but just make sure you do it daily. Freedom follows only when you make productivity your first priority.

Habit 3: Create a Personal Business Standard

Have you ever come home at the end of a long day feeling beat up and tired but not sure what you accomplished? That's because we typically spend our days putting out the fires that seem to break out hourly in this business. Often the only way we gauge whether we've had a good day is if we've put a transaction together or collected a check.

There are very few people who close 365 deals a year, so we must focus on achieving success in accomplishing daily activities, not just end results. The best way to measure the effectiveness of your day is to have a personal business standard. This tool allows you to set a daily goal for the lead-generating activities you want to execute. Thousands of agents in our Coaching program earn six-figure incomes by holding themselves accountable to a personal business standard like the one below.

> *The best way to measure the effectiveness of your day is to have a personal business standard.*

Personal Business Standard	
Calls	5
Notes	3
Pop-Bys	1 (*7 per week*)
New additions to database	1

Make sure your daily goals are clearly defined. Using a calendar, place a huge "W" (for win) on the days you hit your personal business standard. As a wise man once told me, "What gets measured gets done."

Habit 4: Take action

I've seen many agents paralyzed by perfectionism. Wanting to do a task flawlessly, they never get beyond the first step. Of course you want to do a good job, but you have to do it in the time that's available to you.

Newer agents are especially plagued with paralysis by analysis. Often they are indecisive and unproductive because they feel they don't have the experience to take action. But they can't gain experience if they don't ever take action!

This is real estate sales, not brain surgery. If you make a mistake nobody is going to die, including you! And if you are a veteran agent stuck on a production plateau, you have to make a break with your usual business methods in order to achieve better results. In short, you must take action.

Although there never seems to be a "perfect" time to make a call to a potential client, call anyway! You may feel the Item of Value you are giving to your valued clients isn't quite right for everyone. But give it anyway! You may never write notes to clients that they'll treasure forever. But write them anyway!

When you take action, you will be well on your way to winning the day. Or as the Nike slogan says, "Just do it!"

Habit 5: Learn to value each day

The psychology behind winning the day is based on understanding the importance of each individual day. Often we falter in achieving goals because we fail to appreciate that small steps add up to big results. When people are in debt, they can be very casual about assuming more debt because they feel they're already in so far over their heads. Or in trying to lose weight, we easily rationalize that one more slice of pizza isn't going make much difference to our waistline. Similarly, when agents' businesses are floundering, it's easy to fall prey to myriad distractions at the office like surfing the Web, checking e-mail, or talking with the other agents.

We must understand the value each day represents to our business, but winning the day doesn't mean we have to be perfect. During our careers, Brian and I didn't robotically generate leads eight hours a day,

125

seven days a week. There were days that got away from us and days we downright blew it.

In the end, if you want to make your business big, make your focus small. As small and insignificant as one day may seem to your business, it really is the difference between winning and losing. The author Robert Collier once said, "If you think you are too small to make a difference, you have never gone to bed with a mosquito."

Below is a winning formula that has helped many of our clients focus on their goals, maintain discipline, apply a personal business standard, and take action.

The Winning Formula

Daily

1. Write 3 personal notes

2. Make 5 check-in calls

3. Add 1 person to your database

4. Win 2 hours—you win the day!

Weekly

1. Host 2 business lunches

2. Average at least 10 Pop-Bys

3. Attend at least 1 networking meeting

4. Win 4 days—you win the week!

Monthly

1. Send an Item of Value to entire database

2. Make personal contact with all A+ clients

3. Attend a social or business networking event

4. Win 3 weeks—you win the month!

Quarterly

1. Host a networking party, seminar, or gathering

2. Update your business directory

Yearly

1. Host a party for your A clients

2. Get support for your business (see Chapter 15)

3. Win 8 months — you win the year!

Win the Day

After we present at a seminar, participants always ask for more details on how Brian was able to sell 85 homes in one year while working only 35 hours a week, or how I was able to sell over 250 homes in 12 months. There is nothing mysterious about it. We built databases, sorted and qualified them. We sent Items of Value to people in our databases each month. We made follow-up phone calls. As a result, we generated many high-quality leads.

- The one piece of advice we give to every newer agent looking to gain traction: Win the day.

- The instruction we give to the middle producer who wants to earn more commissions: Win the day.

- The suggestion we offer to the top-producing agent who wants more balance in life: Win the day.

- This is the strategy Brian and I have lived during our real estate careers. Do you want to Work by Referral and live the good life?

Then *win the day!*

ACTION STEPS

Revisit the above five habits for winning the day. Decide on three of the five habits you will implement within the next seven days.
(*Circle three*)

Habit 1:   Focus on your GOALS

Habit 2:   Structure your work

Habit 3:   Create a Personal Business Standard

Habit 4:   Take action

Habit 5:   Learn to value of each day

CHAPTER FOURTEEN

Staying the Course: Three Levels of Accountability

BY BRIAN BUFFINI

A man can learn only two ways, one by reading, and the other by association with smarter people.

Will Rogers

If a man empties his purse into his head, no one will be able to take it away from them. An investment in knowledge always pays the best dividends.

Benjamin Franklin

Staying the Course: Three Levels of Accountability

I come from a country infused with water. Besides our streams, rivers, lakes, and the ocean, rain falls on Ireland a good part of the year. Visitors to Ireland often remark on the tranquility of a land bathed in so much water.

Turn up the heat on that liquid, however, and you've created one of the most powerful forces on earth. Steam-driven machinery transformed agrarian societies into industrial ones at the beginning of the 19th century, and today steam catapults F-14 aircraft into the air from ships.

Remember when you started your career and were all fired up to start each day? As your work became routine, you may have lost some of your steam and your productivity cooled to lukewarm instead of red-hot. In this chapter, I'll discuss ways you can recharge your enthusiasm for your work with the assistance of accountability partners, mentors, and coaches. A little help from others may be all it takes to attain your peak performance.

Accountability Partners

Having an accountability partner is a great first step towards turning up the heat and changing your daily habits and routines. When I ask audiences at our live events how many feel they would achieve more if they were held accountable to daily tasks, everyone raises their hands. But the truth is, everybody wants accountability—until they get it.

We've all created excuses for ourselves when we fail to perform as we'd like. And, after a while, we buy into those excuses and rationalize our behavior. As Joe always says, "Almost everyone wants to change their circumstances, but very few want to change themselves."

Joe and I are very driven and focused people, but we both freely admit that if we hadn't had each other as accountability partners, neither one of us would have achieved the level of success we did. Here's the arrangement we had:

We each set daily goals; I would make 15 calls and write ten notes, and Joe committed to making 25 calls and writing five notes. Then no matter how many hours we worked or how many transactions we did, we'd call each other and report our lead-generation activities for that day. If one of us fell short of the goal, the other would ask, "What kept you from 'winning the day'?"

Mentors

A mentor is a guide, a role model, or a trusted advisor. Unlike an accountability partner, a mentor is not a peer. Accountability partners often possess strengths and weaknesses that complement yours. But a mentor is typically someone who is further down the career path from you, has experienced the success you hope to achieve, and has a willingness to share his or her insights with you.

> *A mentor is typically someone who is further down the career path from you, has experienced the success you hope to achieve, and has a willingness to share his or her insights with you.*

In business, a mentor might be your broker, manager, or someone who has built a significant business outside of real estate. In spiritual matters, a mentor can be a pastor, priest, or rabbi. In your family life, a mentor can be a parent, uncle, aunt, or even a grandparent. For financial issues, a mentor can be a financial planner or investment consultant you admire.

Rather than requesting that a person become your mentor—which is akin to asking for a prom date—invite him or her to lunch and ask:

- What have been your best decisions (pertaining to his or her area of expertise)?

- What are the biggest lessons you've learned?

- Give a brief overview of your current situation and ask, What advice would you have for someone in my position?

If I were to list all the people who've taken the time to impart wisdom to me at a lunch appointment, I'd need 20 pages of acknowledgments at the front of this book. Many successful people have helped me during my journey in America. Because having mentors over the years has been so important to me, I took great personal satisfaction in creating Buffini & Company's Certified Mentor Program to help others as I have been helped. In just the last three years, 6,000 brokers, owners, and managers in 15 countries have become Certified Mentors. These role models facilitate our 100 Days to Greatness training program, which has graduated over 40,000 agents (who average six transactions during the program).

Coaches

A coach is a highly trained professional whose job it is to instruct, direct, and encourage a person to achieve at his or her highest level. Unlike an accountability partner or mentor, which is a volunteer role, a professional coach gets paid to motivate you. In the area of fitness, for example, an accountability partner would be your workout buddy, your mentor might be the local gym rat who is in great shape, and your coach is the personal trainer you hire to help you reach your health and fitness goals.

> *A coach is a highly trained professional whose job it is to instruct, direct, and encourage a person to achieve at his or her highest level.*

Buffini & Company has coached over 45,000 agents and lenders, the vast majority of whom come to us through referrals from our clientele. The personal stories you have read in this book have been those of our ClubNet Coaching clients.

We have a team of extraordinarily dedicated professional Business Coaches who are highly skilled in challenging, persuading, and motivating our clients to tap into their fullest potential. And the results speak for themselves. According to the National Association of Realtors, the median income for agents and brokers is $42,600 per year. For agents alone, the median income is approximately $30,000 per year. In comparison, an agent currently being coached by Buffini & Company averages $192,000 annually—six times more than the national average.

And although our specialty is Business Coaching, we also hold our clients accountable to the goals they've set in other areas of their lives. For example, 97 percent of our ClubNet Coaching Members have a written personal financial budget compared to 3 percent of the national real estate population. What does a personal budget have to do with Working by Referral? Everything! If your finances are in chaos, that shows up in every transaction or interaction with a client. For example, it is very hard to focus on what's best for your business and your clients when you are desperate to make a sale to pay your past-due bills.

Our Business Coaches may also help clients attain their personal goals of taking days off work or spending time with family. I've received many notes over the years from the children of our clients thanking us because dad came to all their games that season or that "Mom no longer answers the cell phone during dinner."

Many agents we coach, when referring us to their friends, will talk about how we've effected not only their business success, but also changed their entire life.

Christin Jackson of Chandler, Arizona, credits ClubNet Coaching with laying out a clear business strategy which allowed her more time with her children. At 42, Christin was driving herself hard, raising four children between the ages of 4 and 10, working full time as a flight attendant for America West airlines, and investing in real estate with her engineer husband, Kerry. She longed to spend more time at home with her children, so she decided to get her real estate license, thinking that her work schedule would be more flexible. But Christin soon found out that the promise of unlimited income on a completely flexible schedule was not reality in the daily grind of unstructured real estate. Often, the time Christin planned to spend with her kids evaporated as she worked long hours trying to drum up business and worried into the night about failing.

After attending a Turning Point in 2003, Christin immediately signed up for ClubNet Coaching. Her main goal at the time was not greater production but to achieve better balance in her life. Coach Kim Ortega helped channel Christin's energy into creating a Working by Referral system that gave her more structure and direction. At the end of her first full year of coaching, this rookie closed 52 transactions while working less than 35 hours a week, and spending the quality time she yearned for with her children.

This significant boost in income created an opportunity for Christin's husband to quit his engineering job and join her in the business. Christin was able to further reduce her time spent in the real estate business to spend even more time with her kids. Today their income is triple what it was when they both had full-time jobs, and the quality of life their family enjoys is priceless.

Our ultimate goal in ClubNet Coaching is to embody the both/and approach, allowing Working by Referral to support the client's definition of living the good life. It's important to note that Buffini & Company Business Coaching is not the only game in town. You need to find a coach that meshes with you and understands your goals.

Whether you choose an accountability partner, mentor, or coach, with a little help you can harness the power of your untapped potential, embrace your talents, and become truly successful.

ACTION STEPS

- Find a fellow agent who will be your Accountability Partner. Arrange to meet and discuss your lead-generation goals at a designated time each week.

- Check to see if your Broker or someone within your company is a Buffini & Company Certified Mentor.

- To learn how a Business Coach can accelerate your production and bring balance to your business and your life visit www.buffiniandcompany.com.

CHAPTER FIFTEEN

The Next Step Is Yours

Think left and think right and think low and think high.
Oh, the thinks you can think up if only you try!

Dr. Seuss

The most effective way to do it, is to do it.

Amelia Earhart

The Next Step Is Yours

Our intention with this book was to provide you with an introduction to the Working by Referral system as well as a step-by step guide to putting it into practice. We also hope we encouraged you to not only reevaluate your current business operations but to imagine your ideal career and life. Our desire is that you will apply the Working by Referral system and, in doing so, will experience your version of the good life.

We have countless stories from our live events, digital training programs, and our Business Coaches of how Working by Referral has helped people make lasting changes in their businesses and in their lives. Are you next?

A Word from Joe

When I present, I always tell audiences about Otto the gorilla, the biggest and most beloved attraction at the Brookfield Zoo in Illinois. As the story goes, it was July 1 and the staff was preparing for the Fourth of July holiday, which drew the largest crowd of the year. Unfortunately, Otto was sick.

The panicked zookeeper came up with what he thought was a brilliant idea. He offered $100 to a young employee named Billy to wear a gorilla costume and pretend to be Otto for the big day. Billy, who had just been hired to clean out the elephant enclosure, thought playing Otto would be a step up, so he agreed.

"Just don't do anything stupid," the zookeeper told Billy. "Otto typically lies around all day, so don't get carried away."

Early on July Fourth, Billy put on the gorilla costume, lumbered over to Otto's favorite spot in his enclosure, and stretched out on his back the way he'd seen Otto do every day. For the first few hours, the crowd oohed and aahed over the sleeping primate.

But Billy soon became bored and sat up, looking at the crowd. A great gasp of excitement went up from the audience. When he stood up, the people cheered. Five minutes later, Billy started banging his chest and moving around with more energy than Otto had shown in some years. The excitement of the crowd was palpable. The cheering and shouting brought even more zoo visitors to the gorilla enclosure.

Billy was loving his 15 minutes of fame, and the applause only motivated him to do more. He climbed on the rocks, stomped his feet, and waved his arms. The crowd reacted in unison with a crescendo of cheering and screaming that inspired Billy to take his impersonation to even greater heights. He grabbed a rope hanging from the roof of the enclosure and swung back and forth.

The crowd was euphoric. Never had they seen such a show. Otto was truly a star and the applause just kept growing louder and louder. Billy's enthusiasm soared as he swung with all his might. Like a giant pendulum, he swung high—and somersaulted right into the adjoining lion enclosure.

As he tried to recover his composure, Billy got up on all fours and found himself staring into a pair of blazing eyes and giant fangs. He began to scream for his life: "Help! Help! Get me out here!" Suddenly the lion hissed, "Shut up buddy, or we'll both lose our jobs!"

The point of this story is that there are times when we feel we're imposters and that everyone else has his or her act together. But the truth is, everyone has feelings of insecurity and self-doubt. In every agent's and lender's career, there have been worries that they might not have what it takes to make it in this business. Brian and I often felt that we didn't measure up, and we leaned heavily on one another for moral support. Fortunately, the belief we had in one another helped shore up our confidence and restored faith in ourselves.

Successful people also fight through their fears and doubts by taking action. And with each action, momentum builds—eventually turning into genuine confidence. One of my greatest joys today is inter-acting with people who I know have conquered their self-doubts. Their courage in facing their challenges inspires me to do the same.

So when nagging doubts enter your mind, keep your eye on your goals because on the other side, there's not just a better business, there's a better you.

A Word from Brian

In 1995 I walked away from my daily work of selling real estate, which had been a big part of my identity and success for a long time, and launched a new venture called Buffini & Company. My goal was to help people benefit from the things that had meant so much to me. My com-pany's mission statement is, "To impact and improve the lives of peo-ple," which also happens to be my personal mission statement.

One of the most rewarding aspects of my career today is receiving notes and letters from our clients telling us that Working by Referral has changed their lives. You don't have to be Joe Niego or Brian Buffini to become successful with Working by Referral. We don't want you to be us; we want you to be who you are. This system is a guide for running your business while letting your individuality, personality, and talents shine through.

Real estate is a demanding business. Joe and I have the deepest respect for the courageous people who make the commitment to become self-employed without guarantee of income, benefits, or safe-ty net. Selling real estate is entrepreneurship at its finest—and it offers the fairest form of compensation. You'll get out of this business exact-ly what you put into it. It doesn't matter if you come from humble beginnings like Joe or I did, whether you're an immigrant, or what color your skin is.

Real estate's been very good to me. It has allowed a poor immigrant to build a business that built a fortune that built a life. My hope and prayer for you is that you'll pursue your business with vigor, steadfastly apply the principles of Working by Referral, put on your white hat daily, and enjoy the rewards of living the good life.

Brian Buffini

Brian Buffini is chairman and founder of Buffini & Company. Born and raised in Ireland, he immigrated to the United States in 1986 and entered the real estate business in San Diego, California. Rather than follow the transactional lead-generation methods, Buffini developed a sophisticated framework to grow his business 100 percent by referral. This system shaped over the generations of the family busi-ness in Ireland, helped him forge strong friendships with clients. This ability to generate a predictable supply of high-quality referred leads enabled Buffini to devote his time to providing clients with first class service rather than in advertising or prospecting.

Buffini quickly became a top producing agent. After several years of achievement and success, he started Buffini & Company to teach these systems to others. Today, thousands of real estate agents, lenders and service professionals across the nation are implementing Buffini & Company Referral Systems and the outstanding training program, 100 Days to Greatness.

Buffini has provided expert training to more than a million people through his nationwide Turning Point™ seminars. Clubnet™—the nation's number one business coaching program—has real estate agents and lenders member worldwide. As of this printing, these members average six times the production of their NAR peers.

As Buffini says, "A good coach is able to help get more out of you than you can get out of yourself. Everyone gets better with a good coach." To arrange to have Brian speak at your company event contact Buffini & Company at 800-945-3485.

Joe Niego

Joe Niego, who grew up on Chicago's South Side always had a love for hard work and real estate. Alongside his brothers, he was a star college basketball player and was the second draft of the NBA Houston Rockets. *Sports Illustrated*, the *New York Times* and USA Today are just a few of the publications that covered Niego's story. His career was also the subject of a feature story with Connie Chung on NBC national news.

At the end of his playing career, Niego put the same drive and determination into his real estate career and excelled in national real estate companies as a top producer. In 1992, he met Brian Buffini, and the two quickly became best of friends. Together, they developed systems to proactively generate referred business. During this time, Niego wrote the famous Mayor Campaign Dialog that is now used by tens of thousands of successful real estate professionals across the nation.

In 1994, he started Niego Real Estate, which has since grown to become a remarkably successful office. Using these referral methods, he has sold more than 2,500 homes to date. "Our referral systems provide a step-by-step blueprint for achieving both success and a balanced life," says Niego. "The thousands of success stories across the nation demonstrate that very clearly."

Once again joining forces with Brian Buffini, Niego now teaches powerful lead-generation systems to real estate and service professionals nationwide. To arrange to have Joe Niego speak at your company event contact Buffini & Company at 800-945-3485.

Additional Resources

To learn more about products and services
for individuals and organizations based on
Working by Referral visit:
www.buffiniandcompany.com
800-945-3485

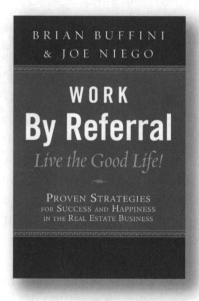

For information about
additional copies and
discounted bulk sales visit:
http://www.workbyreferralbook.com